SHINE

Embrace Your Full Potential and
Live Your Truth with Passion

Helena Goodwill

BALBOA.
PRESS
A DIVISION OF HAY HOUSE

Balboa Press books may be ordered through booksellers or by contacting:

Balboa Press
A Division of Hay House
1663 Liberty Drive
Bloomington, IN 47403
www.balboapress.com
1 (877) 407-4847

Because of the dynamic nature of the Internet, any web addresses or links contained in this book may have changed since publication and may no longer be valid. The views expressed in this work are solely those of the author and do not necessarily reflect the views of the publisher, and the publisher hereby disclaims any responsibility for them.

The author of this book does not dispense medical advice or prescribe the use of any technique as a form of treatment for physical, emotional, or medical problems without the advice of a physician, either directly or indirectly. The intent of the author is only to offer information of a general nature to help you in your quest for emotional and spiritual well-being. In the event you use any of the information in this book for yourself, which is your constitutional right, the author and the publisher assume no responsibility for your actions.

Any people depicted in stock imagery provided by Getty Images are models, and such images are being used for illustrative purposes only. Certain stock imagery © Getty Images.

All illustrations in the book is owned and created by the author.

Print information available on the last page.

ISBN: 978-1-9822-2027-3 (sc)
ISBN: 978-1-9822-2029-7 (hc)
ISBN: 978-1-9822-2028-0 (e)

Library of Congress Control Number: 2019900767

Balboa Press rev. date: 01/21/2019

To you,
all my brothers and sisters around the world
who long for more in life.
I deeply admire your compassionate hearts.
May you now nurture your own needs and dreams
as loyally as you nurture those of others.
May you now claim your full potential and shine bright.
I believe in you.

Contents

Your energy makes people smile. It is so beautiful, joyful, caring, and wise. Thank you for being you.

Welcome Home to You, Beautiful

We are made for loving. If we don't love, we will be like plants without water.

—Archbishop Emeritus Desmond Tutu

Every moment in front of another human being, is your chance to change to world.

—Robin Sharma

No, you're not broken. You never were. You're *perfect* just as you are. Take that in, all the way into your heart. Undress all layers of doubt that have been placed there along the years. You don't need to be fixed in any way, shape, or form. You simply need to be more *you*, to allow for *all* of you to be seen and loved for all the beauty you truly are right here this very minute. We're all loving beings, and we've come here to help and uplift each other. When you inspire and serve others in your own unique way, doing what you truly love, life becomes more of a joyful and playful ride of growth for us all to genuinely enjoy.

You have immense potential. You have a strong ability to take things in, read your environment, and understand the symbolic value of things, people, happenings, and situations. At this moment, it feels as if you're not necessarily frozen, yet you're not taking action either. At least not in the way you long to do. Your inaction is rather frustrating for you to deal with. You're holding yourself back, though you know you have this longing and an immense flood of insights and views that need to be shared.

There is a higher vibe within you that wants to be explored and expressed, but you're holding yourself back for some reason. So at this moment, it's more like you're censoring things, reading things, taking things in, noticing things. And at the same time, it feels like you're half. There is a lot of flow in the side of you that involves sensing, feeling, and experiencing. Meanwhile, the side of you that involves taking action—acting out your desires, dreams, and passion—is sort of just lying there, waiting for you to take that step, to open up and share the fire with the world that is you. That fire flame within you is so wow! If you had any idea of how inspiring you are as a person! Let it out! When you get the balance you long for and that liberating feeling of flow, it will be such a relief for the entire system of you: your body, mind, and soul.

It seems as if you're holding back because you have feelings of not being fully worthy, of not being allowed or good enough or whatever it might be. While the core of you knows this isn't true, there are still those old thinking patterns within you that keep holding you back, preventing you from fully taking action. You *know* you have an important message for the world that you're supposed to share. You know exactly what it is. You need to share it, and you're encouraged to start now.

Your time is limited. Everybody's life is limited, yet so many of us live our lives as if time were endless. And in a sense it is. But this life—this you, this person, this body—is limited. Your time here, in that sense, is limited. Your soul is limitless, yes. Your time in this body of yours is limited. None of us know our exact expiration dates. It could be today or a week from now. Trust that you came here to leave a mark, to leave a legacy, and to contribute positively to this world by being all of you.

Bring out that passion within you. Let it out! You'll gain so much more; you'll be surprised by all the pleasant bonus effects, I promise. Simply live your truth. Live your most inspiring and genuine story. Live the dream that whispers in your heart. Give yourself the permission you've been waiting for. It's time. You know this already, and you can feel it with your entire being. You're probably smiling while reading this. You know what I mean. You don't need a guru to tell you anything. You have such a huge amount of life experience, as well as this inner knowing, combined with your unique gift. You simply need to rest in your own truth.

People have always come to you, sharing their stories, telling you their secrets. They confide in you because they can *see*. They see that you know, that you understand, and on a soul level, they *know* that you *know*. On a soul level, they know they can trust you and that you have wisdom and compassion beyond this lifetime. Share it! It's time.

And while you shine and live your truth, you inspire others to do the same thing. Share your stories, your wisdom, your joyous passion. Most important, share that fire within! That fire is so lovable. Share it. It's time. Now. Today. Make space for you; take that space in a loving and powerful way. Own all of who you are at the core of your being. Trust that you're safe to express all of you. Trust in your ability to flourish at whatever you put your mind to doing.

You have a lot of joy and playfulness within you. You're also very intelligent, and you have reflective skills you could apply to nearly any subject. You could get into any discussion and you always contribute big time to nearly whatever topic, as long as it's resonating within you, with the core of you and your values. Still, when you're just being you, you have this glow around you that radiates joy. You have the joy of a child within you, this playfulness and ability to see beauty in tiny details. That's a secret gift that you have—the gift of seeing beauty in all things, in all tiny details, which makes an enormous difference. You're a powerhouse. You're a powerful lighthouse while simply being you. Shine your light, friend! It's indescribably beautiful for the rest of us to see you shine in all your authenticity.

Somehow, you seem to need a reminder about your intuition, your gut feeling. Trust that first impression of a situation, of a person. Simply trust what you already know and feel. You'll save yourself a lot of time if you just stick with that gut feeling of yours. It's just a tiny adjustment you need to make, yet trust it. That time you save needs to be dedicated to acting on your needs, dreams, and visions. That time needs to be spent bringing your story and message to the world in whatever form it may be.

This side of you—to be active and create movement by taking action—needs stimulation. It's like a muscle; just keep working on it. You don't need to run a marathon in one go. Simply get started and act. Take tiny actions one at the time, every day, and you'll get the balance back. Once you're back in more of a balanced rhythm, between inspired action and restoration, you'll be all right. Even if you hit a bump (you know, life happens, and you might need to interrupt whatever it is you're doing), it'll be easier to get back on track like an athlete.

The longer an athlete has a break due to an injury (or whatever the reason), the harder it becomes to get back in shape and back on track. It takes more time and more effort. This is why it's important for you to be consistent and keep the movement going by taking tiny actions every day. You know what to do. Trusting your gut feeling helps you create a more fulfilling life and simultaneously frees up the space you need right now to truly flourish. Instead of giving second chances because you want to be nice and understanding, simply trust your gut. You know. You already know. Give yourself credit for your built-in and brilliant truth detector: your intuition.

Your energy makes people smile. It's so beautiful, joyful, caring, and wise. Thank you for being you. Keep shining, and show more of yourself to the world, because the world longs to see more of the beauty you are. Perhaps more important, *you're* waiting to enjoy more of the beauty you are. Do you hear it? That nagging whisper within? That inner knowing that gently and persistently asks you to walk your own path, the one you've always felt curious and excited to embark upon. Do you hear it? Be still. Listen. What's this whisper telling you? Allow this whisper to grow louder. Pay attention and listen to it daily.

This book is an invitation for you to create a loving and safe space for yourself, a space which includes *your* needs and desires, as well as your truth. I'm here to hold your hand and be your most devoted cheerleader and loving companion along the way as you step fully into the amazing potential of you. I believe in you. It's time. Let us do this together. Give yourself permission to shine. Not only that, but also give yourself permission to shine *brightly*. Turn up the volume of you. Turn up the volume of your amazing love, passion, and potential. It's time. You already know it is. Lately, you've merely been dipping your toe in the truth of who you are: your passion, your potential, and your authentic expression. This book is your personal cheerleader and companion as you dive deeper into your authentic dreams and potential. Know that you're allowed to live your truth.

Keep in mind, though, that any knowledge and insight that you gain are only valuable when they're consciously and consistently *applied* and *acted upon* in your life. So, you're being encouraged to actively apply whatever insights you might gain on the journey of reading this book. *You* hold all the answers to what is right for you in your life. This is an invitation for you to consistently acknowledge and act upon your own inner knowing and longing.

Oh, and one more thing before we get started! I would like to invite you to read this book *actively*: read with a pen nearby, write in the margins, underline sections and sentences that vibe with you. Use a journal to write down your thoughts, answers and reflections. Discuss it with your friend, partner or someone else that feels right to you. By expressing yourself through writing, speaking, or both, you make things more tangible for yourself. This way, you'll get the absolute most out of this book. And that's my wish for you—the best, the most, in all areas of your life from this moment on.

Your sister in authenticity and compassion,
Helena Goodwill

Rest in Love

Know that my love for you is eternal. Rest
safely in my embrace, my darling.

Do you hear it? That nagging whisper within? That inner knowing that gently and persistently asks you to walk your own path, the one you've always felt curious and excited to embark upon. Do you hear it? Be still. Listen.

Ignite Your Sparkle + Define Your True Desires

Wholeness, happiness, and love are your birthright. As a baby there was no part of you that doubted your wholeness. As a result you lit up the world without even trying.

—Rebecca Campbell, Light is the New Black

We are born with only one obligation—to be completely who we are.

—Mark Nepo, The Book of Awakening

You're *so* ready. It's like every fiber of your being is placed in the starting block, waiting for you to take action. Ready, set, and waiting. Waiting for you to say go. Everything is aligned. Everything you need right this moment is available to you. You're waiting for yourself to take action. You're waiting for your own permission to act upon your dreams. You can tell yourself all you want that "maybe once that is finished," or "once I got that in order," and, "once I've got whatever-it-might-be, ready," *then*. Then you'll be ready.

At the same time, you know that this is not true. You're just fooling yourself. You're trying to win time to feel more ready. Yet you're ready, so you're wasting your time. Well, nothing you ever do is ever wasted in that sense, because you can learn something from every experience.

Right now, however, you're wasting the fabulous feeling of actually doing what you truly, truly *love* to do. You're postponing the experience of enjoying that and feeling the magnificence of *you* making it happen. You know, whatever it is that you love doing, you'll *radiate* once you allow yourself to do all of that and continue to do and share more of it daily. We're all here to support, uplift, and inspire each other, simply by being true to ourselves and our passions.

There are so many of us struggling, doing what we think we're supposed to do, what others expect from us. Little by little, we tend to strangle ourselves until our bodies start screaming in some way: with fatigue, stress, tension, a bad back, an upset tummy, depression, or even cancer. The more we ignore these symptoms, the louder the screams from our bodies tend to grow. Any pain, distress, imbalance, or inflammation is a signal from your body that you need to make adjustments. Your body is telling you that you need to *adjust* whatever it is you're doing. You need to adjust whatever it is that you've chosen to focus upon at that point in time so that you can feel better and feel good. Well, not only good, really, but we can start there. When you're not feeling well for whatever reason, that wise body of yours is kindly asking you to prioritize your genuine needs. Know that you're meant to feel fantastic, amazing, brilliant, loving—and loved. Now and always.

You know you're as ready as can be. Otherwise, you wouldn't be holding this book in your hand. It's time. Remember when you were a child and you *knew* that you were going somewhere special. You'd been longing for it for such a long time, it felt like forever, and you were *finally* on your way there. Even though you had no idea fully what the experience would be like, just the feeling, the anticipation and your vision of it, that in itself created an excitement within you. Because this, *this*, was something you enjoyed doing, something you *loved* doing, and you were *so* excited that *finally* this was about to happen.

It's the same way now. It's the core of you who longs for something—and you know *exactly* what it is. Your longing is unique for you. It's something that has been lingering within you, sort of waiting. Waiting for the right circumstances, waiting for the right timing. You keep saying and thinking, "If only ..." And then you come up with a variety of excuses: "Then, I would." Or, "Then, I will."

It's time to cut that sentence in half and keep only: I will. *I will*. The only reason for you to do this is for *you*. It's for *your own* enjoyment. You're meant to thrive and enjoy yourself, your life, your surroundings, your environment, the people you get in touch with—everything. You are meant to enjoy life fully. You're *allowed* to do so. You're worthy of feeling all of those wonderful emotions, of experiencing all of those things that you dream of. You're *worthy* and you're *allowed*. Right here, this minute, decide for yourself: *I will*. Then add whatever it is that you wish to do. Your list of what you wish to do may be long, and that's perfectly fine. It may be short. It doesn't matter. *I will*. That's your commitment to yourself, to your own needs and to your own dreams. It's time.

I'm here to hold your hand for a little while or for as long as you wish. You may return to this book whenever you need to boost your energy, clarity, and commitment. Simply return, read a few pages, or read a section or even a sentence to remind yourself. This book is a reminder: everything in it is simply a loving reminder for you to shine, for you to turn up the volume of *you*, so that everyone can see more of what a brilliant, loving, wonderful human being you are. So that you can serve the world in the way that you've always longed to do.

You don't need to know every step of the way just yet; you just need to commit: I will. And allow this "I will" to keep growing until it's so strong and unwavering that it becomes nonnegotiable. A firm, loving *I will*. Commit to a loving relationship with yourself and your core longings. As with any new relationship, it requires dedication, energy, love, time, investment and balance to thrive and make progress. You know this, and you *crave* this.

You know you have immense potential. Immense. Think about it. Think about how indescribably many situations and circumstances that you've mastered in your life. It may have drained you at times, and it might have been a living hell to go through, yet you've *mastered* all of it, *everything* that has come across your life path. Everything! Now it's time for you to master your dream, to master that longing, that *immense* longing within you, to get started and create the life for yourself that *you* long for.

Let go of what everybody else may expect from you: your family, society, relatives, or friends—focus on what *you* long for. Honor your creativity. Honor your dream. Honor your truth. Honor your *I will*. What you long for may be more simplistic or more extraordinary than society commonly advocates. It doesn't matter. Simply honor your own truth.

This is a new path, a new beginning. You've spent most of your life caring for everybody around you, making sure their needs are met: partners, children, parents, friends, strangers, coworkers, costumers, and so on, all of them. Your big, compassionate heart is set on making things better for everybody around you. It always has been. It always will be. It's part of you, of who you are, of your loving nature. It's you.

For you to master this ability within you, you need to also fill yourself up completely, not just a bit here and there. *Completely*. You need to be completely full, vibrating with every cell of your being, vibrating with joy, love, energy, and *fulfilment.* Can you imagine? Can you imagine how many more you can serve? How many more you can support? How many more you can inspire and uplift? Those that you're already focusing upon will benefit immensely: your family and friends will benefit from seeing the glow in your eyes, from feeling the energy of you radiating. And the best part of it? It will all be so easy and natural for you to do so.

You see, when you do something you love, be it surfing, yoga, painting, coaching, healing, swimming, whatever it might be— *time flies.* Your passion requires no effort from you because you love doing it. It's effortless and you feel rejuvenated both while doing it and afterward. You feel fulfilled. You fill your inner cup while doing this. That's your core motivation. That's why you should do it: *to fill yourself up* so that you can overflow and share the abundance of your energy with others. Once you're more present with yourself, you can make more conscious choices rather than simply allowing others to choose *you* and to choose *for* you. It's time for you to step into the leader you were born to be: the leader of love and compassion, for yourself and others. Move forward with trust. Know that you're already on the right path.

You've been struggling in the past, sort of pouring from a leaking cup and trying to help others when you've not been feeling well yourself. You've been trying to help out when there have been other things you would have rather focused upon. You have prioritized the person in front of you who needs your help while feeling low on energy yourself.

No. Enough. Stop it. Stop that habit. That's not the way to go about things, not anymore. You've done it for so long, and you feel the shift within you now. You know that it's time for something new. It's time for you. When you focus on your commitment to *you*—your dreams, needs, passions, and longings—then you'll be *naturally* filled with energy, joy, and love for everybody you meet. So simple. Yet we've made it so difficult for ourselves in the past. Let's create something new together. Here. Now. We're starting something new, a new way of living that can contribute to making everyone a winner.

Do you feel it? This bubbling sensation within you, of *excitement*, of joy, of not yet knowing exactly what is to happen, yet knowing that something big is going on. A shift is taking place. It has already taken place, and you're on the other side where you thrive and shine, just like you were always meant to shine: fully, completely, unapologetically, and lovingly. This is the time to come home to *you*, to show up for and nurture yourself in the most authentic and compassionate way you've ever done. This is where it all starts: *with you loving and honoring you.*

Reflect in your journal.

💜 *YOUR ENERGY RESOURCES* 💜

Think back in your life. What are your most precious and joyful memories? Why?

What is it that lights you up? What gives you energy and joy? What makes you come alive?

What can you do for hours while time just flies? On what occasions don't you notice time going by because you're so *involved* in the activity and so *fully enjoying* whatever it is that you're doing? Name those moments. (Your energy resources are unique for *you*. An energy resource could be something as simple as you being in nature, or you dancing, writing, surfing or talking with a stranger.)

💛 *YOUR TRUE DESIRES* 💛

What are you super passionate about? What turns that passion and energy flow on within you?

When are you high on energy and super engaged? Are there any specific topics that you could discuss for hours? What have you always dreamed of doing (more of)? Name those moments, topics, and dreams. The more specific you are, the more helpful it will be for you.

Reflect in your journal.

💛 *YOUR LIFE PURPOSE COMMITMENT* 💛

If you were able to contribute to others in some major way during this lifetime, what would that contribution look like? How will you know in your heart that your life here mattered? Declare it in maximum two sentences and begin with "I'm committed to—." This is your unique life-purpose commitment. This could be, for example, "I'm committed to empower women who have suffered through trauma," or "I'm committed to serve the world by helping people reconnect with the truth of who they are so that they can live happy, energized, and love-filled lives that make a difference to themselves and the world."

As children, we naturally know what lights us up, and we dedicate our time to doing those activities. Perhaps most important, we go with the flow. We're so tuned in to our emotions as children;

we're so tuned into our wishes and our needs in the moment. When we feel a need to cry, we do so. When we feel pain, we embrace the pain and acknowledge it. We cry or ask for help or comfort. We, as children, are so naturally tuned into who we are—our core truths: our feelings, desires, and needs. We reach out and let our needs be known both to ourselves and to others. We go with the flow of life. We go out on adventures and discover things. We play. We meet new friends. We see every new person as a potential friend we don't yet know. We trust that gut feeling of ours. We trust our feelings about others.

When there's a child around whom we feel connected to, whom we feel we have something in common with, we *reach out* and naturally play and laugh together—in an instant! Watch children. They know. Some may be shy, yet they're true to themselves, and they *see*. The younger they are, the more easily they connect with others and reach out to those around them. The younger children are, the *truer* to themselves they are, the less conditioned they are by parents, family, or society to be living in fear and to be doubting themselves. They live in truth. As a child, you were more inclined to trust the truth of your inner being. Thus, you naturally turned to the activities, environments, and people you genuinely appreciated and enjoyed.

If more of us lived as children and allowed our authentic expressions, it would be such an immense release of tension for us all. We would relax into and stand in our truth. So, you're being invited now to think back to your childhood. What did you most enjoy doing? How did you prefer to spend your time? How did you feel while doing these things? Write it down. How can you reconnect with that loving child within? How can you reconnect with that *true knowing* of yours? How can you pay more attention to life and your own needs and wishes? How can you allow for more playfulness? How can you allow for more authenticity in your life? It's time for you to tune into who you've always been.

Reflect in your journal.

💜 *CONNECT WITH YOUR INNER CHILD* 💜

What activities did you love doing as a child? What made you love these activities? How can you incorporate more of these activities in your everyday life today? Did you perhaps love to be creative, to journal, to be in nature, to explore new places, to climb trees, or to be with animals?

Make a list of all the things you loved doing as a child. Then be specific as to how you can weave such activities into your life now. Create an action plan for how to bring these activities into your everyday life on a regular basis.

You'll be amazed to see the difference these activities will bring to your life today. Truly amazed.

You know that beautiful sparkle of yours that lingers within? The one that shows whenever you engage in something that you love and makes your eyes light up? That beautiful sparkle of yours that makes others light up, simply by seeing you? That sparkle, my friend, is the core of you. You need to embrace, nurture, and protect it.

Sometimes in our lives, we get caught up in the needs of others. We put everybody else ahead of ourselves, ahead of our own needs and desires. In doing so, this sparkle within is still present. You still know that it's there. You still feel this longing for more. You still have those dreams for yourself of how you wish to spend your day, what type of relationships you wish to surround yourself with, and what type of working environment you wish to create for yourself.

Most of the answers were present in your youth. What lit you up as a child is most likely what will contribute to you lighting up more today. As a child, you were perhaps very curious about understanding various insects or spending time in nature. Then as an adult, you most likely find solitude during a walk in the forest or by sitting down by a lake where insects can be found. As a child, you were perhaps engaged in creative activities such as building an environment for your toys to play in, a scenario you built up, constructed, and reconstructed again and again. As a child, you were perhaps designing various things. It could be as simple as cooking or enjoying family gatherings around dinners and barbeques. Then, as an adult, you effortlessly create those environments for yourself and others to enjoy and rejoice in.

To ignite your sparkle is also about defining and putting into words all those things that you've been postponing for yourself, all those big dreams of yours. It could be joining a choir, taking art classes, rescuing animals, starting a company, buying a house, travelling the world, going to new places or begin dating to move toward eventually building the family you dream of.

Whatever it is, say it out loud. Write it down. Define it. This way you can hold yourself accountable. By defining it, you're initiating the process of it becoming your reality. Then take inspired action steps to invite and create that vision of yours. You're free. You're allowed. Act from a place of feeling inspired. You'll always be free to choose your life. Others may not always understand you and the choices that you make; focus on those who do.

Time to create your own reality with intention. What is your core commitment to yourself regarding that longing that has been lingering within you for so long? What is your next step? Finish the sentence:

I will—

How and when can you allow for more playfulness and relaxation in your everyday life? Be specific.

Your Sparkle

Move towards that which lights you up and makes
you vibrate with joy and inspiration. That is your
path. Trust it. You are meant to shine, friend.

Unmask Yourself + Find Your Fit

True belonging doesn't require you to change who
you are; it requires you to be who you are.

—Brené Brown

True connection and true intimacy can only be
found when my vulnerability can meet yours in a
sweet spot.

—Nancy Levin

If you had any idea how precious and valuable you are! A part of
you does know, a tiny (well, a rather big, really) part of you knows.
You've just entered the habit of doubting. And this has become
quite a strong habit in the past few years; a habit of doubting you,
of doubting the value that you bring.

If you're a hundred percent honest with yourself, you *know*! At
the core of you, you know. You know because you've *seen*. You've
seen it! When you do the things you love, when you do the things
that comes so naturally to you, then you see *the shift*. You *see* the
shift in yourself and others. You *see* the contribution. You see
how they're *uplifted*, how they're shining, and how they're feeling
all those precious feelings that we're all longing for and striving

toward, all those feelings that we naturally have when we allow ourselves to be *true* and to be centered in ourselves. You know you matter. Now it's time for you to *feel* it and *trust* it, too.

Whenever those doubtful thoughts enter your mind, notice them. If you feel like it, dig deeper into them. It's not necessary, though, because all your thoughts are simply habits. They've become your habits because you repeat them. In the same way, you may repeat thoughts that support you, uplift you, and benefit the new path that you long to take. As doubtful thoughts pop up, notice them. Then gently replace them with slightly better feeling ones, thoughts that propel you in the direction you wish to go. Support yourself with the same supporting and compassionate thoughts that you would think about and express to a beloved friend of yours, as he or she embarked upon a new path in life.

So, how do you go about this shift specifically? How do you do it? A part of you is holding back out of fear that you'll not be accepted, that you won't be loved, and that you'll not be understood. To be truthful, not everyone will understand you, though those who truly matter will. All those who really need you and the emotions, services, products, and energy that you bring by being nakedly you will understand you. The others might come along, later on. It doesn't matter. You know it doesn't matter.

What matters is for you to feel joyful, for you to feel fulfilled, and for you to feel purposeful. What matters is you going to bed at night feeling, "Yes! I positively contributed to this world. I contributed to others simply by being me." Then you wake up in the morning with a smile on your face, happy to get another day of doing the things you love, things that matter to you. You wake up happy to get another day of exploring life, exploring you, exploring your potential, of having the exchange with others that make you feel inspired, uplifted, and curious to learn and explore more.

It's time for you to shed all those masks that you've used in order not to be seen fully, in order not to be misinterpreted, and to keep feeling accepted by others. Shed the masks that have provided a sense of safety while they've also kept you feeling inhibited. This task may feel daunting, or huge, even, when now picturing all the scenarios that you fear facing. For example, you may fear that the people that you hold dear and value highly will no longer like you or might exclude you from their lives.

Let's be real about this. Yes. Yes, your fear may come true. Time will tell. This uncertainty and vulnerability might feel painful and challenging to endure at times. Most likely so. That's true. However, is it better for you to feel someone's love and appreciation for something that you're not? Do you get the point? Would you not rather feel loved and seen for the truth of who you are? Would not that be an amazing beauty to experience? To see and feel, "Wow, I just exposed myself in a way that I didn't believe I would ever dream of doing, and yet here this person is standing right in front of me, appreciating that! And I see in this person's eyes, that he or she is appreciating who I am with all their heart!"

That's authenticity and that's what you most long for: to be authentic, to show up as you, no pretense, and no masks. Moments of genuine connections tend to live on in our hearts forever. What we all long for is a more vivid, genuine, and expanded expression of ourselves. To simply be and share our love and our natural gifts.

The amazing reward that this brings, of you expressing yourself fully and authentically, is that you find your fit. You find your tribe. You find those like-minded people you can truly connect with, who genuinely understand you. You can build new relationships in which you find a deep and meaningful exchange. This will, in turn, contribute to you feeling even more eager and excited to truly enjoy your life fully. You're not here to suffer.

You're not here to play small. You're here to explore and experience the fullness and ever ongoing expansion of you. You're here to sense, taste, feel, and hear the miracle of life.

I know that you appreciate any person expressing his or her genuine self. When each and every one of us see somebody expressing his or her true beliefs, passions, love, and compassion, we're automatically drawn to him or her. Why? Because they embody and remind us of our core. We all long to make a difference, and to matter. And we all do this already, simply by being ourselves. By allowing ourselves to bring our passion out into this world, we serve and contribute profoundly and effortlessly. This is our most powerful contribution to the world, to unleash our true potential and to serve with love and passion. By allowing yourself to be all of you and to shine brightly, you'll also be better able to handle life in general as you'll feel more centered in yourself and your resourcefulness. Fewer things will be able to rock your boat.

So, how do you start? Where do you start to express all of you? You already know one step you could take that would bring you closer to expressing more of you. This can be made in every tiny conversation and interaction, in whatever medium of expression you wish to use that feels natural to you. You may express it with a friend, a parent, your child, or a stranger. Just turn up the volume of you, a tiny bit at the time. Adjust and peel off those layers and masks previously used in your attempts to fit in and feel approved of.

Actually, at times it might be easier for you to be authentic and start this process with strangers. This suggestion might seem and sound rather contradictory to you. Think about it, though! When you meet someone for the first time, they're drawn to you for some reason (or you're drawn to that person for some reason), and it's an open space as you don't know that much about each other just yet.

So, here is an opportunity and a space for you to allow yourself to be all of you, one tiny hint at the time. Worst-case scenario? This person may walk away, and you may never see him or her again. It wouldn't make much of a difference, would it? Because just a few minutes earlier, this person was not in your life to start with. You see what I mean?

From this point onward, invite and allow new people that you meet to truly see you. Those who choose to stay in your life will do so because they've been allowed to see your authenticity and they relate to and appreciate it. The others? Simply leave them be, because then you know. You know that you're not a good match at the moment. It might change in the future. Who knows? For now, you know what you need to know about your current compatibility level.

As you've initiated the process of opening up and showing more of yourself to strangers (for example at events, during travels, etc.), then you can work your way toward your already existing relationships that you might find a bit tricky. Don't worry. You'll know what to do. Trust your intuition on this. You already know and feel in your gut whom you're safe to share all of yourself with in this initial stage of you unmasking yourself. Moreover, you'll feel strengthened and empowered by being more authentic with strangers. This feeling will pour over into your already existing relationships as well.

Simply start by expressing yourself with people who aren't (yet) important to you: it could be a stranger in a café who asks you about that book that you're reading. Be creative (I know you are). Play around with it, because you've reached a point where you just need to be you, fully. By authentically expressing and being yourself, others will see you, and you'll find this tribe, this circle of people around you, or this network rather, of like-minded people, which you long to be around. Now, I'm not saying that you should support only those who are like you, I'm saying you find energy and support among like-minded people (who share similar interests, dreams and core values), so that you can also contribute to those who are not like you.

Did you take that in? Those closest to you are supposed to be the ones who bring you energy, who uplift you, who bring you that certainty of knowing you can reach your hand out and this person will be there (provided they have the time and energy). They'll take your hand. In the same way, you'll take theirs. You share a profound connectedness. You'll be there for one another and support, uplift, and inspire each other. That's what we're all here to do: to contribute and create a loving community together.

Be true to you. Allow yourself the wonderful experience of being seen and loved for who you truly are, to feel and know that you fit. All the love that you've been pouring out into the world your entire life, you're deserving of it too. Don't you see? Love is the essence of who we are! Are you afraid to be loved in all of your glory, the very same way that you love others? Enough of this holding back now. Allow yourself to be seen and to feel loved and held, by yourself and by others. Turn up the volume of love in all directions, including to yourself.

You're safe to trust others. The only time you're possibly let down by others is when you let yourself down by doubting and mistrusting your own intuition. You have your own navigation system already built in inside of you. You always see the signs, yet you sometimes choose to ignore them. Trust yourself. Trust your intuition. You're safe to trust yourself and others. You already know which people are a match to you. Trust that feeling. Keep the bar as high as your innate worthiness.

In order for somebody like-minded to find you, you need to show who you are. Otherwise, they can't find you. In the same way, you can't find another if they're not showing who they are. Others might get a sense of it, but unless you tell your story, unless you show up authentically, people won't know who you are.

Don't dim yourself. You don't have to stand on rooftops screaming, and you don't need to be literally naked. You just need to show up and genuinely express yourself. It could be to just one person this week. It could be to ten people. It could be to hundreds. It's all your choice. It's about you being genuinely, lovingly true to who you are. When you're true to who you are, you'll feel more relaxed and strong in your vulnerability.

It's a bit of a paradox, to be strong in your vulnerability. When you feel vulnerable in the exposure of your true self to others, you wonder "Will I be liked? Am I worthy when being me fully? Am I loveable?" And the answer is always yes. Yes! Yes, you are! You're so worthy! And when you stand there, showing yourself and being authentically you, there's nothing more for you to lose. In that lies the strength. In you being vulnerable lies the golden gem, because the other is also feeling vulnerable and can relate to you, hence a deeper and stronger connection between you is being made possible.

No matter how much we express ourselves, no matter how much we express our genuine selves to others, we will always encounter moments in which we feel vulnerable, where we experience moments of hesitation. Am I worthy? Am I enough? And we always have the chance to get back on track, to the core, to the truth: yes. Yes, you're worthy. Yes, you're lovable. And yes, all of us are.

Oh, and one more thing. You know that beautiful smile of yours? It's the best indicator ever that you're on the right path.

Reflect in your journal.

♥ EMBRACE ALL OF YOU ♥

In which activities, relationships, situations, and environments do you feel allowed to be *all* of who you are? Begin to name them all.

Where and when do you feel completely safe to be you? What activities make you feel harmonious and refilled? Write them down. These are your starting points, where you can begin to express more of you and slowly begin to expand your comfort zone.

With whom do you feel completely relaxed to be yourself fully? What is it about this person or people that makes it feel safe for you to be yourself? Describe the qualities in this person or these people that make it possible for you to relax fully in their presence. Be very specific. (Chances are that many of the good qualities that you appreciate in them are what they and others appreciate about you as well. Just so you know.)

♥ DROP YOUR MASKS ♥

Write down *one specific step* that you can take today to express more of you. Why today and not tomorrow? Because the longer we postpone something, the more unlikely it is that we actually do it. If the step feels too big to take, break it down into smaller ones. A tiny step taken today is better than none. Get started! What is your one specific step for today? Where and how can you begin to express more of your true self?

What you most long for is you, the true and unmasked you. The amazingly compassionate power within you longs to come out.

Your natural joy longs to be expressed more. All that you long for is already within you. Give yourself permission to dig deep into your genuine desires and dreams in life.

What do you wish to create? How can you be more genuine? How do you wish to feel in your everyday life? What do you wish to experience before you die? Free from intellectual conditioning, free from societal expectations, at the core of your heart, what do you genuinely long for? This is your starting point. With this vision as your guiding star, you're able to navigate toward bringing and building your dreams into reality. When you're in authenticity, joy, love, and your full potential, all the rest will fall into place more easily.

The importance of unmasking yourself is undeniable in your quest for a more fulfilling life. Think about it. Let's just say that you were longing for a love relationship and you knew exactly how you wished to feel in that relationship. I doubt that you would be interested in somebody who's not quite content with life and whose main goal is simply to find a partner. I believe you'd be looking for a partner who strives toward creating and exploring life in joy, someone on a mission to make a difference and contribute, who lives his or her life mission and is true to his or her own core values. In short, a partner who lives from the heart, is generous and passionate, just like you.

For you to be able to find this partner, you need him or her to be striving toward living his or her full potential and exposing himself or herself, right? This is the only way for you to be able to see and feel that this is the one you're looking for and that the two of you are a good match. Well, the same goes for you. In order for your tribe to be able to find you, you need to be showing yourself to the world in various ways and forums. In order for you and your tribe to be able to find each other, you need to shine from the inside out. Allow yourself to shine. The world so needs your joy, your compassion, and everything that's so unique about you and your joyful energy. You lift and inspire others simply by being you.

It's almost kind of cute, the way that you try to protect yourself with various masks for every occasion and every context. It's kind of cute because the brilliance of you so outshines whatever it is that you're trying to put on, whatever you're trying to cover or display to the world. The brilliance of you, the authenticity of you, will always at all times in every way outshine whatever cover up you might use. When you show up authentically as you, in whatever way or state that you're in at the moment, you touch others' hearts.

We're all drawn to authenticity. Why do you think we love babies, children, and animals? Why do you think we love their joy, creativity, and way of embracing life? Why is that? It's because of their authenticity—you know what you get! They're true to themselves, and they're true to their surroundings. You can't trick a cat to cuddle with you unless it likes you and trusts you. It knows. It's the same way with children. They know. If they don't like you, they simply walk away (at least if they have that option), or they play by themselves. But they don't want to be close to you unless they like you and find you at least to some degree on the same wavelength as them.

We're drawn to children and their authentic expression. We're drawn to them speaking their truth, even at times when they bluntly do so and have us go, "Uh-oh! That shouldn't be said out loud!" Well, it should be said out loud, shouldn't it? We feel liberated by their truth, by them speaking and owning their truths. So all of these masks that you put on, all the things about yourself that you try to neatly cover up and keep to yourself—release them! Because all of this clinging and nervousness creates tension, which takes a lot of energy from you. Unnecessarily so.

I know you long for heart-to-heart connections. I know you love them, in whatever form they may come. I know you'd like to invite more of those interactions and connections into your life. Do so by revealing yourself, by peeling off those long-worn-out layers. In your vulnerability and authenticity lies your greatest power and freedom.

As you came into this world as a precious baby, you were as vulnerable as you could possibly be: naked, dependent, and helpless. Still, you've grown. In that vulnerable state, your needs were met. Perhaps not all of your emotional or material needs were met. Yet you grew. You're here today. You grew into an adult.

Vulnerability and authenticity spark something unique within each of us. Somehow, witnessing authenticity and vulnerability in another being tends to evoke a wish to reach out, to be there and connect. Vulnerability and authenticity in another remind us of the vulnerability and authenticity within ourselves. We may put on masks throughout our lives, and we can keep those masks up until the day we die, yet it won't prevent us from the feeling of being vulnerable. Our masks only contribute to us feeling more isolated and lonely in our personal struggles within.

What happens as we allow ourselves to be vulnerable and to be seen and held in that vulnerability by another human being, is such a profound experience. It doesn't matter if that other person is someone you know or not. It could be somebody passing by, noticing you crying and asking if you're all right, sitting down beside you, listening, and simply being there. At times, no words are needed in response, simply sharing the emotion and seeing each other provide such a juicy, sweet space that we all long to experience. A tender moment of connection, of being seen for who we are behind all our masks.

To have your protecting walls up and masks on prevent the world from getting to see and know you on a deeper level. Your walls and masks prevent potential threats to a certain extent. However, you keeping your guard up to keep potential pain away from yourself also keeps potential love and connection away. True connection is only possible when two individuals both bring their guards down and allow their vulnerabilities to be seen and felt. This is how we truly connect.

For you to be able to find your fit, to find your sense of true belonging, of truly being understood, you need to let your guard down. You need to say farewell to your masks. You need to invite yourself into your own life as you are. You need to acknowledge your own beauty and your own uniqueness. Own it. Treasure it.

Allow others to see and appreciate your uniqueness as well. Trust that who you are is what so many others are longing to meet and connect with. They're right now waiting to discover you. Allow yourself to receive. Allow yourself to shine. Know that vulnerability is not necessarily a sign of weakness, although we often tend to believe so and interpret it as such. To be vulnerable is to be authentic. To allow yourself to be vulnerable is to bravely own your truth even at times when this may feel super challenging for you.

What sides of yourself are you most afraid to have exposed? Why?

If you would somehow be able to reveal these sides of yourself in a safe context, what would this mean to you? How would you feel?

I Feel You

To truly *see* and be *seen* by another being is
one of the greatest blessings ever.

To allow yourself to be vulnerable is to *bravely own your truth* even at times when this may feel super challenging for you.

Raise the Bar + Set Boundaries

If you want your yes to have more value, you have
to exercise your no.

—Lisa Nichols

If you're always trying to be normal, you'll never
know how amazing you can be.

—Maya Angelou

What is it about you and your loyalty toward others that makes
it so challenging for you to stand up for and express your
own needs? How come the needs of others always tend to come
before your own? Why do so many of us sacrifice our own needs so
willingly as soon as our presence is needed by somebody else? How
come your genuine expression has been suppressed to somehow
satisfy others?

Your boundaries, emotions, and integrity have most likely
not been fully respected in your childhood, youth, or adulthood.
You've not been given the chance to fully blossom, nor have you
known how to stand your ground at all times. This is something
that you've grown so accustomed to throughout your life. As the
empathic and compassionate being that you are, you naturally see

and understand the needs of others without even blinking. Now that you have every chance there is to create the life of your dreams, you have a hard time fully believing that you actually can.

You're almost like an elephant who has been chained so long that the chains are no longer needed; the elephant is not going anywhere although it's completely free to do so. Please know that these are patterns of your *past*. You're free now, free to be you, free to create and receive your every desire. You're free. Take it in. Take a deep breath and inhale your freedom. Only love and respect are to be allowed into your life and your space. Love and respect.

You need your own presence first, at all times. Others needs are secondary, always secondary, to your own. Although it may sound like selfishness, it's a pure and loving self-care mentality. Neglecting yourself while being low on energy is of no use to anyone in the long run. In the safety instructions on airplanes, why do you think you're being guided to put your own oxygen mask on first before helping anybody else? Exactly. It's for your own safety and your own survival. The same applies to your other needs as well, not only regarding oxygen.

Now, in order for you to expand and allow all of you, you'll need to allow yourself to expand your horizons. You need to raise the level of your experiences. You need to step out of your comfort zone again and again and again. The more you step out of your comfort zone, the larger your comfort zone and the larger you allow you to become. This is important and a much needed shift as you've been playing small for way too long now. In order for you to do this, you need to be willing to leave familiar territories once in a while.

Well, let us be honest here. You need to leave familiar territories on a regular basis; you need to stretch yourself and raise the bar.

Do so little by little, if that's what feels most comfortable with you. It's your consistency that's the key here. If you settle for what is ok instead of what you truly want, it will easily create a downward spiral that will likely feel more and more wrong and uncomfortable to you. Saying no when you need to is an act of self-love. Setting boundaries is a practice of saying yes to you and honoring what you truly want in life. You're here to create a new normal for yourself, a new standard that feels right in your heart.

In some areas you might be confident and feel comfortable enough to actually challenge yourself to take a big leap. When you take that big leap in one area, all the other areas of your life will be affected by it. For example, if you're afraid of heights and step out of your comfort zone by taking the big leap of jumping out of a plane to skydive, immediately after that experience your previous comfort zone expands profoundly. This means that facing and scattering your fear of heights will all of a sudden bring an expansion within yourself and a newfound freedom while remembering yourself soaring high up in the sky. It will bring a new perspective on yourself and life, of all things now being so evidently possible for you.

Imagine being able to think back and know that you did it! You did it while feeling your heart pumping and hardly being able to breathe initially up in the air as you threw yourself out. Then you'll remember the feeling of release as the parachute unfolded and you were slowly diving in the sky, gliding, moving toward earth, feeling one with life. With that feeling and that experience, you've pushed so many other boundaries within yourself and your previous perceptions on things. You've pushed them all by taking this giant leap of faith, faith in yourself and in life holding you.

It's a pleasant wave for you to ride, this liberating feeling of facing your fears and moving through your previous limitations.

So, by facing any limiting beliefs or fears you might have right now, you give yourself permission to expand and grow within as well as without.

While raising the bar for yourself and allowing yourself more space for you, you simultaneously need to set boundaries for all activities, people, and experiences that aren't currently on your priority list. In other words, you need to set boundaries in order for your new priorities to get the time, space, and attention they need. Your main priority is for you to feel as good as you possibly can at any given point in time.

Reflect in your journal.

♥ CELEBRATE YOUR SUCCESSFULNESS ♥

You've come a long way already. In fact, I urge you to look back on what you've achieved already in life and feel proud of this. Do you see it? You're being invited to pause and name all of your major successes in life. Write them down. Allow your list of great successes to grow as long as you wish. Be grateful for and proud of your inner resourcefulness.

Why not do something to *celebrate* your successes too? Perhaps together with some friends or family or both?

Imagine how many people there are in the world, walking a path like you've been walking before them. These people are like different versions of your younger self who would benefit immensely from hearing your story and learning how you overcame your obstacles in life. Wouldn't you love to see them succeed too, and to do so more easily thanks to you sharing your story with them in various ways? I know you would. Otherwise, you wouldn't be reading this book.

You didn't come here to play small and settle for anything mediocre. We all get in life what we consciously or unconsciously choose to tolerate. You have the right to say no. Use that right. If your best friend started dating someone who took advantage of her and her generous heart, would not every cell in your body scream that your friend deserved so much better? Your dear friend deserves nothing but the best, right? Well, the same goes for you.

One who is right for you in your life is one who sees all of you, cherishes all of you, and openly, unconditionally, and naturally showers you with genuine love, respect, care, and appreciation. It's all about mutuality and balance so that you can maintain and elevate your energy. Don't ever settle for anything less than that when it comes to matters of your heart. You deserve everything you wish for and more. Now, you can still upgrade your life and you know it. Please take this in: you deserve the best and only the best in all areas of your life.

Lift your standards, and your spirit will be uplifted. Accepting and tolerating unwanted behavior will always leave an itchy feeling within you, lowering your mood and energy. All of it can be easily erased by raising your standards. It can shift in an instant, really. Be sincere in your emotions, though. Only then will you be able to fine-tune your own alignment with your truth. By being honest with yourself, you'll be better able to nurture those genuine needs of yours.

Anytime you hold yourself back, you're resisting life itself. Holding yourself back is like trying to deny a flower to bloom. Others around you already see and appreciate your blooming. They're simply waiting for you to turn your gaze toward yourself and truly see your own beauty the same way that they're stunned by it. Each time they look at you or think of you, they see your inner and outer beauty so obviously and brilliantly. Most of the time, people already know. Others sense what is going on within you, the same way an entire room can sense the unhappiness of a married couple in spite of them trying their best to keep up appearances. Similarly, true connection between people is felt in the hearts of others observing them. We all know intuitively way much more than we give ourselves credit for.

Know that you're selling yourself short by accepting and in a way even encouraging unwanted behaviors from people around you. What you tolerate will likely continue. Allow others to rise alongside your new and higher standards or simply be let go off. Act in accordance with your wishes. This is how you teach people how you wish to be treated. Keep in mind that this is about you setting standards for yourself. Allow others to have the same freedom of setting the standards appropriate for them. What is true for you may not always be true for someone else.

> Those who make the most noise—symbolically speaking—in your life, are not necessarily the ones who love and appreciate you the most. Some may love you for all that you are and patiently await your attention and presence. Be really honest with yourself: Are you prioritizing correctly? Are you listening to the guiding truth in your heart?
>
> If you had only one week left to live, which relationships would you prioritize? What activities would you devote your time to? Whom would you call? Whom would you spend your precious time with?

Yes, as you raise the bar and let certain people go, there will be a void for a while as you learn to grow used to them no longer being such active parts in your life. Feel this void and fill it with your dreams and energy sources: read inspiring books, take classes, join interesting events, take yourself forward, have fun and enjoy the moment! Free up all that space that they have taken and that you so willingly have been giving away. Every text message, phone call, or social activity spent with energy-draining company is taking valuable time and energy from you and your life.

Note that this doesn't imply that these people are necessarily energy draining by nature. All this means is that you currently fail to experience a feeling of meaningful exchange in their company. That's it. They're good and doing the best they can. So are you. Now, gently create the distance you need from these people and activities. You're done settling. Everything that's not serving you needs to go: relationships, habits, and beliefs. This is your time to shine brighter than ever before!

You're done downplaying your needs and feelings for somebody else's sake. Period. These types of dynamics need to be let go off in order for your life to thrive fully as you've come here to do. You've taken your life to a whole new level, where there's no longer room for these types of relationships. They're done in your life. Let go and do so with love. Write a note if you wish. Write it for your own eyes or send it to the person or people in question. You can also burn the letter, as a symbolic gesture of releasing it. The choice is yours. If you wish, thank for all the good times and lessons learned, then release them.

You're no longer willing to carry the responsibility of others. You simply notice their needs, as you've always been doing with excellence, yet no longer step in unless there is a mutuality of some sort (in the form of energy exchange through rewarding conversations, money, inspiration, etc.). This is the healthiest mind-set for you right now. It's the same with the process of developing a sensitivity to gluten: your body has been exposed to it in such excessive amounts that you can no longer tolerate another dose of it. Same here. Your body and soul have carried responsibility, massive responsibility, for others throughout your entire life. Now you're done.

The time has come for you to say a final goodbye to any person or situation that doesn't benefit your well-being. Stop giving your time, energy, and life away to people who you don't genuinely enjoy being around. Moreover, by taking on responsibility for somebody else that's theirs to carry, you are, in a sense, making them dependent on you rather than encouraging their true potential. Know that no one can ever use you unless you allow them to. Also know that no amount of love or kind gesture is ever wasted. What is wasted in a situation or relationship that doesn't feel like a good fit to you, is your precious time that you may wish to spend differently.

Let go of fantasies of how things could be between you and another person if you're continuously being served tons of evidence of the very opposite being true. Your loving heart is admirable, and so is your willingness to always seek to understand others' emotions and behaviors. You striving to understand another's point of view is a wonderful trait that generally gives you a broader perspective on things in life as well as a more peaceful mind. Just because you understand someone, however, doesn't equate to that person being qualified as someone to keep close to you. When needed, ask yourself if you'll allow yourself to be drawn into drama again or if you've now learned to own your own truth and be free? You know that you crave truth and authenticity nowadays and any mixed signals will inevitably become very energy consuming for you to handle.

Although you have an amazing intuitive gift of seeing someone's potential and most preciously loveable heart and soul, if that person currently can't see that themselves, he or she will keep acting based on his or her own beliefs and convictions. Your intuitive ability to see his or her core self and innate value help that person trust him- or herself and his or her value more. As a potential client of yours, this is priceless and life changing. As a friend of yours, this is uplifting and immensely rewarding.

At the same time, it requires a level of authenticity that few are accustomed to or fully know how to handle. As a matter of fact, the closer anyone gets to you, the more challenging it will be for that person (and perhaps for yourself as well) to handle your authenticity and deep love, depending on how willing and able that person is to meet and see his or her own truth and value. Some will act out, be disrespectful (although they're mainly disrespectful of themselves), withdraw, be unreliable and unpredictable, only in attempts to buy themselves more time and space to try and catch up with you. No need to judge this. Try to observe with loving eyes. Hold a loving space for yourself and others.

We all carry the ability to relax into our authenticity. It's a matter of choice: of daring to throw ourselves out into unknown territories and to trust that life, love, and those we love will hold us. When truly loving yourself, you know that you'll always catch yourself and that others and life will always do so as well. When not fully loving yourself, you doubt your own potential and loyalty toward yourself. Thus, you doubt the intentions and reliability of others (and life). Allow your love for yourself and life to grow stronger. You deserve it. You were born to enjoy it fully.

Whenever your joy and energy fades, adjustments need to be made. You know your own path by the way it feels. Trust yourself on this. Trust your own body and emotions to always steer you in the right direction. Make sure to remember this for as long as you live: you're of no use whatsoever for anybody in this world when you remain in a state where you're losing your energy and joy. Whenever you notice such an imbalance, be it because of your current circumstances with your work, your partner, or a friend, you know that it's a signal that a change is needed. Step away, objectively observe the situation or relationship, and then make adjustments according to your new insights. Do this with the highest respect for your own truth and values.

It's of utmost importance that you always remain true to yourself while simultaneously striving to understand the perspective of someone else. Act for the highest good of all, which always includes honoring your own needs and wishes. Always. When you're operating from a level of fullness and abundance, you contribute to others effortlessly and naturally. To lose energy and joy for another is not an act of help; it's called *codependence*.

Begin being more mindful and selective about the company you keep, and be fully present in your relationships, especially the relationship with yourself. You've been the nurturing parent to so many others around you, yet hardly fed yourself anything but mediocrity. You're your primary caregiver and caretaker. Nurture yourself the very best you can in every single way possible.

You're the expert when it comes to giving second chances, though there is no need for this, especially since you seldom stop at the second chance but rather continue for too long providing these chances. All these chances that you're giving away are precious opportunities denied yourself. You see, when you give those second chances yet remain the same standard, nothing really changes. However, if you wish to continue to give people second chances, there's one element, a crucial one, that needs to be implemented in the process. Raise the bar and stick to it as you give one second chance to someone. Allow the other to raise his or her standard of how that person chooses to treat you (and others) or simply leave your life. No drama needed in the process.

You see, if your standard and that person's standard are a match, he or she will continue to be a part of your life. Since you're your most important caretaker and caregiver, the standards you set will determine the quality of all your relationships. Remember your own worth at all times and fill yourself up first. Then you can share your overflowing love, energy, and joy with others. Don't abandon yourself any longer. Embrace yourself. Pamper yourself. Pay attention to your every need and fulfil it. Nothing selfish about this. It's called self-care. This is your time to come home to you and fully support yourself.

Take command of your own life. Let go of the people pleasing tendencies that at times render you feeling dragged like a rag by others. Rather, lead yourself and make active decisions on how you wish your days to unfold. Stop allowing others to pull you in different directions and most importantly: stop allowing others to pull you into their drama and negativity. To live the authentic life that you dream of requires focus and energy, two ingredients easily lost in environments containing drama and negativity. People are not always aware of having this effect on you; they're simply doing the best they can, given their circumstances.

Similarly, you've not always been fully aware of allowing others to pull you into their drama and negativity. Yet you've been given clues and tiny hints in that you may have been feeling down or tired after talking to or seeing them. You see, your body and feelings are always communicating with you. Pay attention to your body whispering so that you don't have to endure it loudly malfunctioning and collapsing in various ways. Be selective of your thoughts, surroundings, and relationships as they set the foundation for your growth and expansion.

You see, we teach the very best by being a living example of what we wish to teach. Whatever you wish to teach and help others with, you need to do for yourself as well. Authenticity is highly inspirational and transformational in the sense that it allows all layers of masks, shields and people pleasing behavior to fall off and allows for the true inner beauty to shine brightly for all to see and connect with.

The kind of people you truly want in your life are the ones who step up and show up when needed, the same way you now show up for both yourself and others. You've spent all your life being the strong one in your relationships, holding it all together practically as well as emotionally with your compassion and commitment. Now it's time for you to keep being the strong individual that you are and to also be allowed to be completely vulnerable as well while being in committed relationships with equals (friends as well as partners). It's time and you know it.

Be honest with yourself regarding what you want in life, what you long for, and how you feel. Tune in to your feelings regularly, pay attention, and ask yourself: "How am I feeling right now? Is there anything I can do right this minute to lighten my mood a bit?" At times, you tend to suppress feelings of disappointment and even excuse others' behavior as perhaps not being all that bad. Please, stop that behavior of gold-plating unwanted behaviors. They're not right for you. Period. To look for the best in others is a wonderful quality, really wonderful and actually life changing for others around you as well as for yourself. You help turn lives around by seeing and supporting the very best potential that you see in others.

However, you don't have to allow people that leave you feeling low on energy into your intimate and closest circle of relationships. Love them from a distance. Honor their potential as well as your own space and energy by maintaining a certain distance until their level of potential has shown some evidence of manifesting into action. In other words, this is their qualification into your space. Yes, they need to be worthy—they need to honor your worthiness the same way you naturally honor their worthiness and potential from the very first minute they step into your life. Please note that this doesn't imply that they're bad people; it simply means that they're not currently a good match to you based on your core values. This may change later on; time will tell if your compatibility has the potential of improving or not. For now, honor your truth.

Learn to say no to all things, people, and situations you don't truly want, regardless of the nature of your relationship with the person or people in question. It doesn't matter if this person is your friend, partner, relative, a potential partner, a customer, your employer, or even a stranger. Saying no doesn't mean that you're unkind, unloving, or aggressive. Saying no means that you respect yourself, your values, and your boundaries. A no can be said in the most loving and calm manner, yet be all so powerful in its clarity as you say it.

Love yourself enough to say no to unwanted behavior. You deserve to feel loved and safe at all times, nothing less. You get what you tolerate. Raise the bar and let others raise up to your new standards or fall away from your life. You know what you deserve. Listen to your feelings—they serve as your true compass. If there is something that doesn't feel good, it's because you deserve so much more. Trust it. Know it. Act accordingly.

This is phase two of your life. This is the next level. This is you stepping up to you: your dreams, your longings, and your potential—fully! This is you creating the stage for yourself. Your life is your vivid, conscious stage for you to create, and be the true voice of your heart, so that you can connect with all those around you that you're meant to get in touch with in this lifetime. Be it through text, film, stories, online, or live, the format doesn't matter. What matters is the connections, the bonds, and the energy of creation. That's what matters. This is about taking yourself and your innate worth seriously. You've contributed big time already in your life. Big time! By being so compassionate, by being so loving and looking to the needs of others. You've contributed big time already.

However, you've done so by putting yourself last and putting everybody else and their needs ahead of your own. This, my friend, is your time to combine both, because you're a compassionate being and you'll continue to always be a compassionate being! The big difference now is that you'll always, from this moment on, give yourself the very same compassion, the very same love and commitment, that you've given to others. You'll give it to yourself. You're worthy of enjoying the same awesome level of commitment from yourself too. You're giving it to yourself already this moment. You've made the shift and from this moment onward, you fill yourself up. You now focus on your own needs simultaneously as you serve others and contribute to the lives of others.

It will feel like you've been upgraded by doing so, because you'll provide such vibrant energy to everybody around you. You feel it. You know it. It's a pure joyride to value and nurture yourself right now. Although you don't yet know all the things that are to come, you do know that they're what you've been inviting. Everything that will come into your life now will be of the greatest service to you and others. This is the magical, truly magical, experience for you, as you're now devoted and committed to yourself and focus one hundred percent upon this. You're committed to your *I will*.

This commitment is so massively important that you now choose to say no to all those distractions and all those energy-draining activities and relationships. You've been taking an honest look at all those distracting habits that you had created for yourself in the past. You've finally admitted to yourself the behaviors you've previously chosen so as not to feel and acknowledge what was going on within you at the core of your soul. Keep stepping up and stepping out of the distractions around you.

By focusing exclusively on what you do want in your life, by naming it, believing it, and allowing it, you make it happen! You make it happen the very same way you made everything else happen repeatedly in your life until you learned the lessons hidden within these experiences. There will be more lessons to be learned repeatedly throughout life. This is part of growth, and you're always a work in progress. Luckily, you've now come to learn one of the most important life lessons: you're worthy of living and experiencing exactly everything that you long for and dream of and more.

Be proud of yourself for trusting your own wisdom and worthiness now. Be proud of yourself for lovingly letting go off past disappointments, blaming, and people-pleasing habits. Be proud of yourself for choosing love, ease, flow, and clarity for yourself and others. Enjoy being a conscious creator of your own life. There is so much magic within you.

> You've now raised the bar for what you'll allow in your life. What specific boundaries do you need to set to honor your new standards?

Reaching Higher

In a flow of love and truth, giving and receiving
abundantly. Joyfully spreading my precious wings.

Love yourself enough to say no to unwanted behavior. You deserve to feel loved and safe at all times, nothing less.

Find Your Focus + Say
No to Distractions

You can be distracted or you can be legendary, but you don't get to do both.

—Robin Sharma

♥

Trust your inner voice so much that other people's opinions are appreciated but not needed.

—Phil Good

♥

How **easy it is to lose track of our dreams** and how equally easy it is to find them again once we choose to focus on the right priorities for ourselves. There is a constant stream of various impressions and potential disturbances going on around you, constantly available for you to distract yourself from what you most need to focus on. Depending on where you are, there will be different flows of distractions coming your way.

It can come in the shape of text messages on your phone, phone calls, or you mindlessly scrolling on social media, glancing through emails, drifting off by watching meaningless drama on

TV and keeping busy with unimportant chatter. Chatter, chatter, chatter. Sometimes you do this consciously; sometimes you have this itchy feeling within, like a restlessness or impatience, and you can't really figure out why. You're simply not at peace and you can't seem to find that harmony within. So you keep on distracting yourself with various things. This could even include activities such as going out having a drink with a friend (it doesn't really matter if you have a drink or not). You hang out with people, and you may enjoy yourself at the moment, yet it's not a fulfilling experience. It's just empty chatter. You're not present, and that's the core issue here.

Allow yourself to be fully present with yourself and people around you. Allow yourself to be present with whatever it is that you truly, wholeheartedly wish to focus on. This is what is of importance here: for you to be truly authentic and present with yourself, with your emotions, with your longing, and with your greatness. For you to be inviting in, accepting, and expressing the wholeness of you is to fully embrace the magical experience of life. Allow yourself to do so with the same curiosity and excitement as a young child.

In order for you to be allowing your greatness and your expansion, you need to say goodbye and no to distractions. You need to make conscious choices of showing up for yourself, of showing up for what it is that you're here to be and do in your full potential. You're not here to be mediocre. You're not here to play small. No! That's not for you. That's not for anyone, really. Yet the focus is on you right now, because when you start giving space for yourself, you're allowing others to do the same thing. So, it all starts with you, right here, right now.

When you reach an older age and look back upon your life, wouldn't you wish to feel within your heart that, yes, you did it!

You did everything that you most preciously dreamt of doing. You did it—each and every one of those things that you longed for. Whenever you fulfilled one dream, a new dream emerged.

A new longing will always emerge, and you'll embark upon that one and the next one. You'll always keep growing—that's what you're here to do: you're here to grow, to expand, to enjoy life, to bloom. You're here to shine, and it's time for you to focus— truly, wholeheartedly focus—all your energy and be very delicate and very specific in what you say yes to. Find and fully own your voice. Own and use both your yes and your no. They're equally important. In fact, the nuances of the language you use affect your life immensely. Feel the difference between "I have to finish this project" and "I'm committed to finishing this project." Also feel the difference between "I don't know what to choose" and "I'm exploring my options." The first versions indicate a lack of power, whereas the second versions declare you being in the driver's seat in life.

Therefore, I encourage you to carefully, specifically, and delicately choose your words and thereby choose your focus. Declare for yourself: "I hereby choose to do this. I long to do this, and I will do this." Then say: "Because of me wanting and committing to doing this, I will say no to the following things that I'm currently doing." And name them.

Whatever it is, name them so that you know specifically what it is that you'll no longer waste your time doing, what you'll no longer distract yourself with. It's time to stop hiding from your potential, mission, purpose, and your core longing. When you embrace this core longing within you, you'll feel fully alive and fully energized. When you're fully energized—wow—you light up, and you also light up those around you, like the positive, loving, uplifting supernova that you naturally are.

Do you feel it? By stepping into the feeling of doing this, by allowing yourself to be specific and get clear about what it is that you truly want in this moment, do you feel the peace, harmony, joy, and passion that come from this? Can you feel how your entire system begins to relax? There is no stress, because you've been very clear on what you say yes to and what you say no to. More than that, you're entirely free to change your mind whenever you wish.

Among the things that you say no to, some of them will be things that you say no to for the rest of your life. It could be habits, people, working environments, situations, hobbies, thoughts, habits, limiting patterns, or routines. Some of them, you just minimize. And some you simply reschedule, like "No, I decide to respond to this at a certain time later on instead of immediately responding," or you disengage: "I choose not to do this at all, because this is not serving my energy and my focus right now."

This process is yet another layer of allowing yourself to be you, of consciously stepping into the leading role of you and deciding for yourself what it is that you wish to do. Whenever somebody calls or asks something of you, before responding, you check in with yourself: "What do I want? What do I need to focus on right now? Does this, whatever it is that's calling for my attention right now, need to wait?" Be very, very conscious and powerful in your decision making and trust that you're worthy here and now to focus on what is important to you. Because what is important to you will bring about very important ripple effects in immensely positive ways to so many around you. You see, it's not all about you. Yet it starts with you. Here. Now. Do it. Commit! Commit to you and your true longings. Now. The world is waiting to enjoy your bright, shining, smiling face and your caring heart to an even greater extent, and so are you.

Reflect in your journal.

❤ *FIND YOUR FOCUS* ❤

Now set your intention. Travel in time for a moment. Travel to a place where all good things are possible. Picture your ideal future one year from now. Remember that all things are possible.

- What are you doing?
- How are you feeling?
- Who are you surrounded by?
- How do you spend your days?
- Where do you live?
- What are you grateful for?
- How do you contribute to others?
- Which of your dreams are now reality?

Write it down on a piece of paper in whichever size feels good to you. It's of utmost importance that you write in present tense while creating this list or vision board to make you truly feel it come alive in your mind. You're allowed to be very specific when writing this. This is your own genuine vision for yourself. It all needs to ring true in your heart and bring you a feeling of joyous excitement. Make sure to devote time and focus to writing this vision down.

Once you're done, put it in an envelope. Write the date one year from now so you know when to open it. Set a reminder on your phone if needed or write it down in your calendar. One year from now, you read your vision. You'll be amazed at the accuracy level of it. I promise! If you wish, you may write yourself a new vision each year.

By committing to this vision of yours, you're committing to you! What steps will you start taking now to allow this vision to become your reality? Write them down.

Reflect in your journal.

♥ DEFINE YOUR DISTRACTIONS ♥

Define (and be very specific): what makes you lose your energy, focus and time? What are your main distractions? List them all. Then be super specific in how you're going to minimize or eliminate these distractions. Write one column with your main distractions and then outline in the column next to it how you'll minimize or eliminate these distractions from your life.

Make these lists as long as you need them to be and be as specific as you possibly can. This is for *your* sake that you're doing this: to give you clarity, focus and direction.

At times, you may distract yourself in order to avoid certain feelings lingering within you. There are moments when you consciously or unconsciously try to numb and distract yourself from your own truth, feelings, and core longings. The best indicator for when this occurs is when you don't feel happy or calm after an activity but rather feel an uneasy restlessness within. You know you're craving authenticity, so honor that. Honor your own longing.

Sit with your emotions and put an end to the previous pattern of distracting yourself from fully feeling them. To distract yourself is to deny your truth and to keep yourself imprisoned by unhelpful habits. You may meditate, journal, exercise, or whatever activity that aids you in connecting with your inner processes. Admit your own truth to yourself so that you can own it and share it with your surroundings. Your truth will set you free, and its ripple effects will inspire others to set themselves free as well.

The deeper you sense and allow yourself to sense all of your emotions, the more liberated you'll be. Right now, there's a form of calibration going on within you, a process in which you're allowing yourself to fully own your space, time, and truth. You're gaining clarity on your unique inner radio channel by moving away from disturbing signals and restoring your focus on you. You're reclaiming your worth. You're adjusting to the liberating and empowering feeling of acknowledging and committing to your compassion for your own needs and passions. In doing so, you simultaneously shine and serve all your sisters and brothers in the most inspiring and uplifting way possible. Zoom out from pointless chitchat and disturbing vibes and allow for yourself to go deep with yourself and your feelings. The deeper you go within, the higher you'll help elevate yourself and others. Stay focused. You've got this. Trust it. Know it. You were born to do this. You're the owner of your stage in life: you decide the design of it and who is to be allowed and invited in to take the stage with you.

You're numbing yourself with distractions. It's like you're shying away from looking at your full potential, of looking yourself in the mirror and appreciating, seeing, acknowledging, loving the beauty of you and everything that you're capable of. To some extent, you would rather divert your attention and distract yourself with pointless—truly pointless—activities, such as browsing through Facebook for ages and ages or watching series on TV or pointless magazines that bring up the same issues again and again and again. You distract yourself in so many ways, which is a waste of your creativity, potential, time, and energy. To break a habit requires a lot of dedicated discipline. That's why a genuine tribe to engage with and a mentor to inspire you could be very beneficial for you in this process. Who and what we surround ourselves with influence our focus and energy. What inspires you will likely bring out the best in you.

You've had people-pleasing tendencies of always putting others ahead of yourself. You've done so because you're a caring and giving person. You've wanted to be there for others (and you still do). Parallel to this, you've had intense dreams and longings within that you've held back, pushed down, and ignored. The process of you ignoring those dreams and putting yourself last naturally stirred up feelings of disappointment with yourself. However, you can look at it from a different point of view. You may have let yourself down in the past, in the sense that you've put yourself last. All that's required now is that you make your commitment to yourself your number one priority regardless of what happens around you.

You're your number one priority from now on so that you can fulfil whatever it is that you've committed to experience in this life. Be brave enough to cut the distractions off. Some of these distractions you can cut off completely, and some you can minimize. It's all up to you and the extent to which you wish to be loyal and devoted to yourself in the very same way that you've been loyal and committed to everyone around you that you care for. Allow yourself to see the brilliance of you. Allow yourself to focus on that longing lingering within you. Nurture it. Protect it. Care for it in the very same way that you would care for a newborn baby. Be attentive to your needs.

Such a strong part of you, such a bold, big part of you, longs to expand, to grow, to keep discovering new sides and new strengths within you. Yet you're holding yourself back a bit in that you distract yourself by engaging in numbing and pointless activities that simply consume your time and energy and add nothing of value to you. These activities don't bring you the sense of fulfilment, excitement, growth, and expansion that you so long to experience. You have these conflicting feelings within you in the sense that you on the one hand long to experience this while at the same time there is fear involved. There is a fear of not being good enough: Am I really all of this that I so long to be? Am I capable of bringing this to life? Am I worthy?

Along this path, you'll have moments where you tend to divert your attention from your goal. They'll fade eventually, or they'll at least be less regularly occurring. At the same time as your goal and your dreams excite you, they also bring up this fear as you're moving toward unknown territories. I would warmly recommend that you approach this with the same curiosity and consistency a child does in learning to walk, in getting back up there, in allowing yourself to have setbacks or have less rewarding days.

Setbacks don't mean that you're less qualified or that you don't have it in you. Setbacks simply mean that you need to keep showing up for yourself. In doing so, you need to be very determined—crystal clear—with yourself: What is the most important mission for you right now? What is the most important project or activity that would truly help propel you forward? How and when will you devote your time and energy to this? How will you integrate it and prioritize it in your daily life?

If you look at your life today, you'll see that there are so many things that you wished for in the past that are now present in your life. It could be that amazing apartment or house that you're staying in, the satisfying career that you embarked upon, that soul-fueling journey you went on. There are so many things that you've brought into your life by focusing on them, be giving your attention to your own priorities and longings. This is a process that you need to be dedicated to, that you need to be consistent with in order for you to keep growing.

To be fair, you can't ever stop yourself from growing and evolving; it's a natural process. However, it's the same way with you as with a plant. If you put a plant in the best environment, suitable for that specific plant (as some enjoy shade and others enjoy immense sunlight), it thrives. Whatever is right for you, whatever environment that brings out the best in you—this involves the nature, surroundings, relationships, activities, hobbies, wakening hours of the day, books you read, films you watch, music that you listen to, lyrics that you sing along to—all of this feeds you. What is right for you feeds your soul, your dreams, and your growth.

By focusing on what feels best for you, what brings energy and nourishment to this sparkle within you, many positive ripple effects will evolve around you. This can involve improved sleeping patterns, unexpected work opportunities, new relationships with like-minded people, increased income, more relaxation, more meaningful encounters with strangers (who may become new friends), improved health, and so on. So, as you give nourishment to yourself, which is specific to you (the nourishment you give an orchid is not the same kind that you give to a cactus), it increases and brings forth more of you and your vitality. (You can find your personal nourishment in your answers to the assignments "Your energy sources" and "Your true desires"). It will bring energy to your step as you walk through your day and as you engage with the people around you. You'll feel lighter and more fueled when you choose to truly nourish your soul and your entire being.

This is your main focus: to nourish yourself in the best way possible. This focus will bring forth a sense of stability within you. Life will be forever changing around you in the same way that you're forever changing and evolving in your growth and your abilities. There will be a major shift, though, in that when you focus on your growth and your sparkle within, it will bring a stronger sense of being grounded, centered, and energized (you recognize your inner sparkle by that feeling in your heart that says, "This is the true path and choice for me"). You'll no longer feel as easily swayed by life into diverting energies, soul-sucking careers, or draining relationships. These phenomena will no longer have access to your focus and energy in the same way that you've allowed for in the past. You'll see the shift so clearly as you look back upon your life one year from now.

This habit of you distracting yourself is perfectly fine. It's part of your path. Yet be aware of what it is that you're doing. Be aware of the patterns that you create for yourself whenever there is some important thing at stake for you. Will you be willing to receive? Will you be willing to openly be experiencing and allowing for the good stuff to come to you? The good stuff that you wish to experience and be a part of, will you allow it to enter your life?

As you distract yourself, you're numbing yourself, sort of closing your energy and narrowing your attention span. You make yourself unavailable to all the truly juicy stuff when you chose distractions. Open up. You're worthy, and it's time for you to put all that energy, joy, love, and devotion into your main focus and your commitment into your specific *I will*. You created that *I will* for yourself; now show yourself that awesome loyalty that you've mastered in relationship to others. Master it with yourself now as well. It's your time to shine, as simple as that. Give it to yourself! You're worth it. It's time. Agreed?

Can you see it? That admirable loyalty that you've had toward others and that you still have toward others? However, you're being more selective in whom you're giving your loyalty toward these days, which is brilliant! Well done. You've also been taking very bold steps lately toward being true to yourself and making yourself a priority. That's so awesome. Some ten years ago, wow! You've come such a long way. Now give yourself credit for all the shifts you've gone through. Give yourself credit for it. Show yourself what a true master creator you still are. Allow yourself for a moment to visualize the feeling of this *I will* being true already. Visualize it being present in your life. Visualize it being already here and already your reality. Close your eyes. Visualize it. Feel it. Feel it with your entire being.

Do you feel the excitement? Do you feel the joy it brings? Keep this feeling alive and act from this state of being. Act from a place of it already being true. You've brought so many seemingly impossible tasks into solutions. You've brought so many difficult and challenging times into resolutions and peacefulness. You're capable of almost anything. You know this, right? Well, you're capable of everything—let's not fool anybody! Decide for yourself what you wish to bring forth in your life. Keep adding to it as you go along creating it. Keep expanding. Keep focusing on what brings you joy and what brings you this feeling of being alive, of truly making an impact and continuously expanding your horizon. Allow yourself to discover more of you and more of the world at the same time.

You're such an inspiring being. Your compassion and your caring heart have healed so many along the path of your life. You have no idea how much your actions have rendered immense gratitude around you for your presence. You've moved people to tears out of feeling loved and seen for who they are. You've helped people rise again and again in times of despair. Your helping hand has been the only sign of hope and love that made all the difference in a moment of isolation and loneliness of another. You really have no idea of the magnitude of your contribution to the lives of others simply by being you. Your love transforms. Your caring heart will always be treasured, remembered and loved.

Allow yourself to fully feel the significance and importance of who you are and what you have to bring and share with this world, what you have to offer. Allow yourself to feel all of your brilliance, to own it, and to share it. In focusing on you and your vision and dreams, you allow your brilliance and potential to unfold fully in the way it was intended to. Allow yourself to bloom.

If you were to enter a relationship with a partner of your dreams, you would do so with full commitment and focus. You wouldn't allow yourself to wander off and distract yourself with random admirers. You'd make sure to take excellent care of yourself and strive to always show up at your best. Same thing if you were to start a new employment or a new career; you would make sure to show up each day and give the tasks your undivided attention. You would bring out your inner genius and embark upon each new task with enthusiasm and full commitment. Right now, you're recommitting to your relationship with yourself. Do yourself the priceless favor of bringing out your inner genius and your outstanding loyalty in your commitment to yourself. You'll be forever grateful toward yourself for doing so.

Honor your time and energy as the divine gifts that they are. Your energy, focus, and time are available in this moment, never to return again. The time that you're given now will never be returned to you. When you ride a bicycle, you need to maintain your focus and your balance to keep going forward. If you get distracted and keep looking in a direction other than that in which you intend to go, you'll not be able to see whatever might appear on the road of yours. This could be fatal. You could get wounded. Your bicycle could get damaged. You could potentially die from an accident. I'm using this analogy about your potential and your life purpose right now, as your distractions affect your authentic vibe and energy.

If you keep distracting yourself by, for example, constantly being there for others and neglecting your own needs and dreams, you will, in a sense, die a little. You'll be living in your body, you'll be living physically, but your soul and your inner being will be feeling kind of dead if you keep distracting yourself for too long. You distract yourself from what is true for you. So it's super essential for you to keep honoring your own needs and priorities, the ones that you've named and claimed upon this journey that we share together right now.

Whenever you aren't in pleasant mood or space, acknowledge that for yourself. It could mean you saying to yourself: "Hang on a second. I'm doing this distracting activity again. What am I turning my face and attention away from by focusing on these distractions? What is it that I don't face by doing this distraction instead?" It could be some uncomfortable emotions that you're avoiding, or new priorities that feels challenging or overwhelming to you. Whatever it may be, allow yourself to be really honest with yourself. What are you trying to avoid or sooth through distractions?

It's a challenge to keep showing up for yourself, because you've been trained to neglect yourself for others throughout your entire life. So, this is a shift. It's a major shift, and you can do it. You're doing it already. You're doing brilliantly in this process. Allow yourself to become more and more aware of your own patterns. Kindly ask yourself: "What am I trying to run away from? Why do I keep distracting myself with mindless activities? Why do I fear plugging myself into me, into that sweet flow of feeling fully alive from the inside out?" You already know that whenever you allow yourself to go there, to the place of your authentic sparkle within, you thrive.

Let's say you love riding your bike, and then you stop riding it for a period of time. Then it likely becomes a bit of a mental hurdle for you to get back in the saddle. Still, you know that, once you take your gorgeous butt and place it up in the saddle again, you'll enjoy a sense of flow. You see, riding a bike is a very good example here, because maintaining the balance, finding the right amount of movement to keep going steadily, as well as knowing when to rest, is essential in life. You can still raise the bar for yourself whenever you wish, absolutely. You know that once you get going and get into shape, you can ride longer distances and keep a higher speed at times. It's the same thing in this process. Focusing on your commitment to you is the same kind of ride. You'll master it. You'll find new ways to show your own brilliance to yourself.

Know that in a very near future, you'll notice the former distracting activities and people pop up around you now and then. You'll smile with satisfaction when this happens, as you'll notice the difference within yourself that you no longer get triggered to answer the call from these distracting activities and people. You're on the right path. Trust it. It's yours. That's what makes the whole difference: you're walking on *your* path, allowing yourself to go in the direction of your heart's desires, and in doing so, you're sharing so much love with others. Be proud of yourself. You're doing brilliantly. You sure are. Truly brilliantly.

To give your focus and attention to those people and activities that are not one hundred percent right for you (that you notice yourself losing energy when being around or engaged with) is like having a hole in the gas tank of your car. You'll not reach your maximum performance level or your full potential when there is leakage. When you allow yourself to say no to distractions and maintain your focus, magical things will start to happen. You'll see this for yourself. You will. It's a given. Trust this.

What changes have you made already to improve your focus?

How can you celebrate these changes, so that you boldly encourage your own victories?

You Are Magical.

When you focus on what you love, then the entire universe
supports you and showers you with endless blessings.
Receive and enjoy! There is more on the way.

Walk Your Talk + Keep Showing Up

You don't need to see path, you just need to be in the game.

—Michael Neill

A master is a beginner who keeps beginning.

—Mastin Kipp

Do you know why you sometimes feel so sad and low in energy at times? It's because you're not fully acknowledging and owning your true feelings and longings. Whenever you feel low, you're not walking your talk; you're not acting in accordance with your truth within. You're yearning for more. You're settling for crumbs when you deserve to have it all: harmony, joy, love, purpose, and meaningfulness in your everyday life.

Allow it in. It's available to you already. Begin allowing it in. Tune into your own truth, whatever it may be. Regardless if the truth may feel challenging or overwhelming initially, it always liberates and ultimately brings a sense of calmness and peace in your entire being. Staying aligned with your inner truth is like fine-tuning an instrument to optimize its delicate, mesmerizing, and unique sound. Act in accordance with your true longings. You might be inclined to believe that you're settling for crumbs externally: materially, in relationships, in your spare time, at work. This is very likely to be accurate. More than this, though, you're settling for crumbs of *yourself* by hiding the blossoming of your innate potential. There is so much more of you to explore and to experience than you might have dared to fully acknowledge previously. Your daily life is very likely too small for your soul right now. Embrace your full competence. You know that it's outstanding. Use it! Trust your innate brilliance and wisdom as you navigate whatever field and context that you're placed in. Any environment in which you feel a need to hold yourself back or somehow adjust to fit in will always leave you feeling less energetic and joyful. To put any constraint on the natural flow of *you* is very energy consuming even if you may not always notice this effect in the moment.

Remember that a diamond is still a diamond, whether it's polished and sparkling or not. You've always been precious and worthy; the only difference is that now you begin to *feel* and see it too. You know *exactly* how to navigate and prosper in all environments, regardless of the tempo you may have to keep. The only thing required to allow for this to happen is your own permission. The thing is that you know so much more than you give yourself credit for. You often know the needs of strangers simply by glancing at them. Use this skill with yourself as well. Value yourself as highly as you *were born* to be treasured. Stay centered in your truth and your genuine priorities, and you'll glow as intended.

Understand that there is divine timing in everything that happens in your life. Looking back, you'll see this so clearly. Trust that the same is true now as well, even though you're not always able to see the full picture just yet. At all times, seek to remain centered in trust. Worrying is a waste of time, and your time is precious, very precious. Dedicate your precious time on your personally selected priorities in life. Most of your problems in life are solvable if only you allow your own creativity to flow freely. Most of your perceived problems stem from you believing that you're limited and restricted when, in fact, you're always more free than you tend to allow yourself to be. Whenever you feel pressured to walk a walk not meant for you, your body and mind will react and act up. Listen to yourself when this occurs. Pay delicate attention to your own needs and feelings.

There will be days when you step courageously into your powerful potential, and there will be days when you shy away from it. This is perfectly fine. Take tiny, little baby steps, crawl if you must, yet keep recommitting to yourself and your *I will*. Remember that you have the control at all times. You decide at all times. You have the power. Get clear on what you want and need. Express it.

Nearly everything will smoothly adjust to your wishes and highest good. Trust. It all starts with you getting clear on what you want. Focus most of your energy on what you want, rather than your problems. To zoom out from your problems whenever you find them overwhelming is one of the best habits you can create for yourself. This allows for you to shift your focus on what it is you truly want, to imagine a better version and—voila—your creative mind will instantly serve you various ideas on how to bring this imagined better version in your mind into reality! Your vivid imagination is one of your greatest superpowers—use it freely!

Reflect in your journal.

♥ *CLEAR YOUR SPACE TO INVITE THE NEW* ♥

Open up to create the life you so immensely long to create. How are you to welcome something new and exciting into your life when your hands are full of things not truly wanted? Make space. Do this energetically, materialistically, emotionally, and practically. Clear your space. You know that it's needed. How can you clear your space at home? What needs to go and what needs to be brought in?

How can you clear your mind and relax more on a regular basis? What old stories and beliefs do you need to let go off? What empowering stories and beliefs do you wish to replace them with?

What relationships do you feel drained by? How can you actively change these dynamics or lovingly let them go?

Which existing relationships do you appreciate wholeheartedly? How can you nourish them better?

What type of new relationships would you like to invite in? What do you share in common? Where are you likely to find such people?

This is perhaps the most challenging part of it all. Now you've gotten clear on what it is that you wish to do. You're beginning to find your fit. Somehow it now feels like it's all up to you to keep showing up, to keep your commitment to yourself (which is true, of course). This phase of the process, will return again and again as we will forever evolve and make progress in our lives. In this phase, you'll undoubtedly have moments of questioning yourself, and you might procrastinate and digress a bit. You set out on your journey, you get started, and then your energy starts to fade due to various reasons. It could be that you get interrupted or that something shows up internally or externally that perceivably requires your attention. You find yourself once again needing to get back on track.

This part is about you recommitting to you and your promise to yourself. This is a decision you need to remake on a regular basis in order not to fall victim to circumstances. This is where you commit to owning your potential, especially so at times when it feels ultra-challenging. No matter what happens in your life, there are always plenty of things that you can change somehow and redirect, reconsider, or reschedule. You see, this is about responding to your core urge and making it a priority. This is about recommitting to yourself and to your longing. This is a time for you to emerge, to keep showing up and really walk your own talk.

Whatever you encourage others to do is true for yourself as well. You know this. You know how to reignite your sparkle each and every day. Whenever your energy fades, reach out to yourself and listen. What is it that you most long to do? Like if you find yourself being stuck—tune in! Ask yourself: What do I need? What is my truth in this situation? What do I need to do in order to feel that progress is being made? What do I need right now to feel energized and fulfilled? For you to be fulfilled, you need the feeling of whatever it is that you're doing to be genuinely meaningful to you.

Get clear with yourself. You need to be super honest with yourself. Tune in and ask: What do I want right now? How do I wish to feel? What do I need to do to be able to feel that way? How can I shift my mind-set in an empowering way? You already know what would be the best solution for you right now. You already know how to fix it. You already know what you need to do. You don't need somebody else to tell you this (at times, you might need to be reminded of your own awesomeness—that's all). You'll find the time, and you'll find the energy when you make yourself and your potential your number one priority in your life. It's about you stepping up. It's about you trusting that what you wish for is important, that your needs are important. Trust that whatever you need to feel alive and enthusiastic about life is important. When you fill yourself up by putting your needs first, your life will get a whole new feeling of flow to it.

In the process of all of this, it's of utmost importance for you to find the balance between discipline—which in this sense means showing up for what you most long to do—and self-care, which is a prerequisite for you to be able to actually show up. Your self-care is a nonnegotiable. For you to be able to walk your talk, your everyday life needs to be characterized by you tuning in to your own needs, paying attention to and meet them in whatever way feels best for you. Stay committed to your self-care and your dreams. Stay committed to your projects and to creating the way of living that you've always dreamt of.

Turning your dreams into reality requires flexibility and dedication: you sure know how to handle both, because you have that superb level of loyalty toward others. If you've been employed, you've been very dedicated and loyal to doing your very best given the requirements of you. You always outperform the expectations of you. Now use the same dedication, loyalty, and commitment— the outstanding level of commitment and over all high quality that you've been giving to others all of your life, whether it be to friends, employers or coworkers. Give that to you yourself now.

Your commitment to yourself will in turn be so beneficial to others too in the long run.

Some days, self-care can mean you truly pampering yourself with good company, a walk in the park/forest, a moment of meditation, a dinner in your favorite restaurant, travels or vacations. Self-care also means allowing all of you to be seen by yourself and others. Look closely at questions such as, "Why am I doing this?" Self-care requires a self-awareness, to be aware of: "What are my needs right now in this particular moment? What am I longing for? How do I wish to feel?" Your answers could involve something simple, such as longing to listen to a certain song today before going to work or going jogging. Whatever it might be, do your very best to give yourself that space and nourishment.

Whenever we feel stressed or pressured or feel a demand to perform, we tend to reduce or eliminate all those very things in our lives that actually gives us energy, such as self-care habits and hobbies. This is rather ironic, because your self-care should perhaps be regarded as nonnegotiable as your sleep. To take good care of ourselves involves taking care of our bodies as well as our emotional needs each and every day. By nurturing ourselves, we give ourselves the best possibilities to actually commit, walk our talk, and align ourselves with the wishes and desires that we've expressed.

Under pressure, we become performance oriented and thus tend to undervalue the importance of the energy giving activities, habits, and people in our lives. To perform well, we need to nourish ourselves in the same way as racehorses and cars: we, too, need to be kept in motion, have well-needed rest regularly, and be fueled by the best nourishment available on all levels (which includes best food, thoughts, company, environments, etc.).

Walking your talk means that whatever you wish to give to others, whatever service you wish to bring to the world, you need to give yourself first. You need to serve yourself first. For instance, let's say that you need to get a haircut. You enter a hairdresser's saloon just to notice that the hairdresser's hair looks rather unhealthy and rough. Wouldn't you hesitate to place yourself in this hairdresser's hands? Wouldn't you rather go to another hairdresser whose hair is shining with vitality and has a delicately made haircut?

In other words, you need to do for yourself what you wish to give and do for others. You need to do this to feel aligned, get credibility and to make it self-evident to yourself and others that you're walking your talk. Although you may struggle at times (after all, bad hair days do exist) and we can't always be on top, yet we can be honest with whatever challenges we might face in the present moment. By honestly sharing your challenges, you'll be able to continue to show up and walk your talk. Life is a process. Everything in life is a process, which means that you're never really done. This is a good thing as it means that you can always keep showing up. You're invited to enjoy your expansion. You're invited to enjoy life. If you feel that it's your life mission to care for others and to help them thrive, start by helping yourself thrive.

Throughout your life, you've been a master, a true master, at sensing others' needs and being devoted, committed, and loyal to serving them. This is true for your relationships, friendships, partnerships, and companionships. You're one of the most loyal and committed people one could ever come across. However, you need to apply this mastery of yours to yourself. You need to show the same loyalty that you've shown toward others all throughout your life, to yourself now.

The previous steps in this book might have been challenging (not might have been, they most likely have been challenging for you): in revealing more of you, in you stepping into your truth and your potential. However, this is perhaps the most challenging part of the process, of you showing up for you, again and again. This process of you recommitting, each and every day, declaring for yourself in action and words that you're serious about this—in spite of your fears, your insecurities, and all those challenging emotions playing peekaboo within you. You still remain true and loyal to you and your commitment to you. You know you can do it. Yet it's a new path for you. It's your path. You're stepping boldly into your full potential, into your divine and—much longed for—dreams. You're now owning and expressing how you wish to fully embrace life.

This is a special and unique gift, this life of yours. You'll never be given it again, not in this way, not in this shape, not with the same individuals around you. This life is your chance. This is when you become your own master. Nobody can fulfil your dream apart from yourself. You're the only one who can take step after step in the direction you long to walk. You don't need to have it all figured out. Nobody does. All you need to do is remain in motion, which means staying true to you and your emotions as your emotions tell you every single time which direction you should choose. You already know. You always have, and you always will. You always know your truth. Your truth is always your best friend. Your truth is the core of you. Your truth always feels good. It may cause excitement and a bit of nervousness, absolutely. Yet it always feels good in your body to own your truth.

So, how are you to deal with various hindrances that come up for you? For example, hindrances such as when you don't have the time and energy you need or when you start procrastinating. All of these are just excuses, because you know that when you commit to you, you fill find all solutions needed. You're such a creative spirit, and you'll always find solutions and ways that you've not yet thought of. Always. You have it in you. You also know whom to ask for guidance. If you need extra support or guidance, you already know whom to reach out to. Most importantly, reach out to yourself. Your longings are reaching out their hands to you. You've already taken their hands. You've already committed. You know that you won't let go. You know that you'll walk with loyalty and devotion toward seeing your core longings become your reality. You're free. You're free to choose. You're free to walk your walk, whatever that looks like for you.

Remember to be kind and patient with yourself as your system adjusts to your new way of living. It's new and somewhat unknown. Your body and mind are new to this. Your soul knows the way. Feel grateful for your superb antenna (aka your intuition)! Trust your intuition and inspiration to safely guide you each step of the way. You can do this.

Fall in love with yourself and love yourself and your life mission to the extent that you and this wonderful life mission of yours become your priority. No relationship, habit, or situation should ever be allowed to be an obstacle on this path of yours. You're too awake now to ever go back to that sort of behavior. You know it, and you've already felt the shift. Enjoy the new.

Think of it as growth. You grow continuously just as you did as a child. You outgrew your favorite shoes and after a while it became painful and even impossible to wear them. However, they were replaced with completely new ones. The old stuff—your habits, thoughts, relationships, and preferences—that no longer fit who you've become, they will all be replaced with new, fresh, and exciting ones. Make space for the new. Allow yourself to feel the joy of welcoming the new: the new relationships, the new insights, the new habits, the new beliefs and the new experiences that are entering your life.

You'll be amazed by all the wonderful things already on their way to you in this very moment. Enjoy and keep receiving. It's all part of your greater service here on earth: to be a living example of all things lovingly possible. You're magical! Remember that. You were born with your unique skills for a reason—now play with them and spend more time in getting to know them even better. Master your skills; they're meant to serve both you and others favorably.

Whenever your energy is low, you need your own pampering and devoted attention. As soon as your energy is a bit lower, you tend to put the needs of those surrounding you ahead of your own. This often renders you completely depleted. Don't be so hard on yourself for doing this, though. You're always doing your very best given the circumstances. All you need to do is adjust and begin giving yourself better feeling thoughts and experiences—one single step at the time. No more, no less. Let go off what has been. Place your entire focus on the life that you wish to create for yourself. Start telling the story of your new life the exact way you want it to be. Get clear on your vision and let this vision of yours become your guiding star and align as many of your thoughts and actions toward it as you possibly can. Also know that what used to make you feel happy and energized may no longer do, as your energy has shifted. Fill yourself with the new.

All the brilliance and all the enjoyment and heartfelt moments that you so generously wish for others to experience, so too are you meant to experience this. So too are you to experience the truth and the full potential of who you really are. All of you: bruises, marks, shadows, whatever you wish to call it. All of it is to be embraced, loved, and seen by you and life.

You see, whatever we experience in life, regardless of the depth of the challenges that we're facing throughout our lives, they're gems in disguise. The challenges that we occasionally experience are precious gems, because in the process of moving through and past them, lies great wisdom. This is divine insight and precious wisdom that we discover and that we're meant to share with one another.

These experiences have two sides to them. First, there is a challenge which you move past and through. Then, as you turn around and look back, you view the experience from another perspective: from the perspective of having survived, of having endured and thrived through the process. That perspective aids you in gaining more knowledge about yourself and understanding how you dealt with it and what you learned in the process. That helps you to elevate and place yourself on a new level of understanding.

When you're to face a similar experience again, you'll have that wisdom and extra knowledge based on your experience. This will, in turn, help you embrace the new challenge with an extra set of muscles and extra expertise. When you incorporate what you've learned and you put this to use, you walk your talk. Walking your talk means putting all your experience and wisdom to use. Whatever you read, whatever you experience, whatever you learn from others, if you don't put it to use, it's wasted. It's a complete waste of time and energy if you don't put it to use in your everyday life.

Use your lessons, your knowledge, and the true inner knowing within you, your intuitive guidance system. Listen to it! Listen to your own knowing. Listen to your own wisdom. Take those steps: giant leaps when you're in a state of flow, tiny steps when you feel a bit of resistance. It doesn't matter in which pace: keep showing up for yourself, each and every day, so that you'll feel fully alive. Do this so that you'll keep feeling that extra surge within yourself to be in tune with your own desires and callings in life.

You already know so much. You already know. Period. You always have, and you always will. You're reading your environment accurately all of the time, yet your habit of doubting yourself clouds your perception. Trust your intuition unconditionally. It's only a matter of plugging yourself in and trusting your intuition and inner wisdom. Trusting your intuition will help propel and guide you forward. We've all been equipped with a delicious guidance system within: our intuition. That combined with our experience: wow!

When we trust this, when we trust ourselves and we trust life, anything is possible! To be able to rest in and trust the truth of who we are is such a liberating and uplifting experience. We long to rest in the authenticity of ourselves and those around us. By doing so ourselves, we invite others to do the same: to blossom and to own their full potentials. To show up for yourself is a matter of showing up to your needs, your feelings, and your truth in every specific moment. To show up isn't necessarily a matter of taking action and being pushy, although movement contributes to you maintaining your balance. These combined forces of progress, so to speak, of rest, rejuvenation, and movement is seen in nature as well. The movement is the ever-changing motions and emotions and the ever-changing flow within and without.

Acknowledge and tune into questions such as "How am I feeling today? What are my needs today? How may I increase my energy in this moment? How can I fill myself up today, so that I can serve the world with my overflowing energy, joy and love?" Whatever you wish to do for others, you now also to do for yourself. You are your own most trustworthy partner in life, each and every day, attentively listening, playing, and loving, like the most compassionate friend, partner, parent, sibling you could ever be to yourself. You show up and you keep showing up. You came into this world to shine and to be all of you. Keep giving yourself permission to do so.

Our children are our role models. They don't have to force it; they just naturally shine and glow. When all their basic needs are met, they giggle, play, and explore! Life is our playground. Our life is our stage. We're free and worthy to create whatever we wish at all times. Set yourself free and keep committing to yourself and your dreams every single day! Keep showing up for yourself. Be as loyal to your dreams, needs, and visions as you have throughout your entire life to the dreams and needs of others. They all matter. The dreams and visions of others matter immensely. As do yours.

It's easy for all of us to withdraw, give up, and hide in the face of challenging times. What is one step that you could take today that would make you feel enthusiastic and energized? Write it down and go do it. Now. The world needs you, and you need you to show up for yourself and the world, simultaneously. You've got this! Now go do it. This is a commitment that you've made, remember. To yourself. Now go honor the truly wonderful, brilliant, and amazingly compassionate being that you are. The rest of us love to see your eyes sparkle, and will be inspired to allow ours to do the same. Let's shine, sparkle, and radiate together, shall we?

What do you need to keep showing up?

How can you make sure that this need will be met?

Do you perhaps need a mentor of some kind? If that's the case, then who, when, and how?

Astonished

Explore the miracle of life with the curiosity and
openness of a child. So much magic awaits you.

Tell Your Story + Serve Others

Often, it's what happens to us in the darkness that
help push us into the light so we can let our light
shine.

—Vishen Lakhiani

♥

You could never possibly know who's waiting on
you to be courageous so they can be too.

—Amber Lilyestrom

♥

There is a liberating power in an authentic narrative. When
we own our authentic voice, we're given a context, a sense of
wholeness in which we're better able to understand the details in
a new light. By striving to make something tangible for someone
else through narration, we simultaneously make it more tangible
for ourselves.

There are stories all around us. Stories that transform, uplift,
and encourage us to become aware of our own narratives. There is
immense power available in words. Think back to when you were
a child: There were likely stories read to you at bedtime. There
were perhaps stories told by grownups about your childhood and
at times also about the lives of the grownups surrounding you as

well. There were stories of how you were perceived by others when you were a baby and young child. There were stories about the environment you lived in and stories about life. All these stories, along with your experiences, have shaped you. Now, here you are, grown up and free. Free to use your own voice. Free to have your own perspective on things. Free to be you. Free to claim your own narrative. You're free and encouraged to inspire others with your personal story.

You know already that so many individual stories have come and gone in your life. Some came to stay. Some came to be retold and shared with others. All the books you've read. All stories that have left an impact, big or small, on you and your life. Teachers that you've met. Mentors. Friends. Children. Relatives. Strangers. Their stories all touch upon your life in some way. Similarly, your story matters. Your story will serve to inspire others greatly. Your voice matters. Your unique passion and your unique experience matter. You see, your story matters even as you're silent. It shows. Your story shines through. Most people already sense what it is that you seek and long to express.

Imagine for a minute that you're about to enter a room filled with twenty people. Everyone in the room is quietly waiting for an event to take place. You're to join this little crowd, already knowing that you most likely share a few interests in common with some of them, as you have all come to experience this specific event. Among these twenty people, you instantly notice someone to the right. Her eyes are glowing. Simply by looking at her, you know. You know that you have to talk to her as those eyes speak so loudly while her lips are silent. As the event proceeds, you finally gather the courage to approach her during a break. You both share your views on the event so far. Before long, you start asking her questions and she tells you glimpses from the story of her life. Without you knowing it, it turns out to be just what you most needed to hear at that point in time. You're deeply moved by her words and so is she while seeing your response as she is sharing her story with you.

This, this is what we all most long for in life—moments of connection, relationships, to truly see and be seen in return. For this to happen, someone needs to show a bit of courage to share a portion of his or her life story and his or her own truth. To ask questions and attentively listen is equally important. This is what connects us. This is how we best serve each other. This is how we're given the opportunity to feel "oh, me too" while relating to someone else's story. We feel less alone and more connected. We learn that there are others out there who feel the same way. Now it's your turn to tell your story and help transform this world into a place of more heartfelt connection.

There are few things in life that so strongly unite and connect us human beings as narration and stories. Through stories, we can identify with and recognize ourselves in others. Your unique story is no exception, especially so when you speak your truth, when you speak with passion and speak from your heart. You've come such a long way on your own journey of discovering you and understanding yourself and life. You've come far too long to hold yourself back any longer. Speak your truth. Share your passion. Do so with love, energy and commitment. Tell your unique story. Share it!

In sharing your story, you automatically serve those who need to hear it. They need to hear about your unique journey in your own words so that they can better understand themselves and the nuances of their own journey. Think about it. Whenever you've been in challenging situations in life, hasn't there been someone you know or perhaps someone famous telling you his or her story and thereby filling you with hope that you too will be able to make it through? Even a song with empowering lyrics can evoke this feeling within us. There is no need whatsoever to hold yourself back any longer (not that there ever was!). Whatever it is that you're holding within yourself is already felt by others. They already sense it somehow on some level, so it would be so much easier for you to just let it out. Say it. Name it. Share it.

What is mainly holding you back right now, is your self-awareness. You see, you think that this is about you. You fear that sharing your story, doing your thing, and creating the life that you dream of will somehow be judged. This could be in relationship to your family and friends, partners, coworkers—whomever.

But you see, this is not entirely about you. This is about you owning your voice and thereby simultaneously serving all the people who will benefit from you telling your story, from you sharing your experiences and your unique gifts. Others will be uplifted and inspired. They will find hope.

Seriously, is there anything more beneficial to us in moments of despair than regaining hope? You're a bringer of hope to this world. Doesn't that help you see things from a different perspective? This is not entirely about you. This part is about your contribution to the world, about your loving legacy to the rest of us.

This is the part where you combine all your previous processes in this book. You'll continue to process all of the previous steps as you tell your story. In telling your story, in unmasking yourself, in sharing your core truth and your experiences in life, you'll touch the hearts of others. You'll speak, you'll write, and you'll express yourself in various ways, from your heart to other's hearts. This is where you allow your heart to speak and take charge. You switch your thoughts off (all that mental chatter, puh!). You allow your truth and your heart to connect with others. You do this in whatever way, shape, or form that suits you best. Share your story in whatever way feels most genuine to you. There is no right or wrong way to do it. Your way is the way, you standing in your full potential, you standing in your vulnerability, and truth is your number one strength. This is how you serve the world. As you continue to share your truth, you shine. You light yourself up, and you light up the lives of others simultaneously. You pay it forward.

You're such a compassionate spirit! You're such a loving and caring person. You always have been. No more holding back, friend. Continue to stretch your comfort zone by sharing your authentic story and your unique gift with the world. You see, your gift is not for you to hold onto. Your gifts are meant to be delivered, and you'll know exactly who needs them as you recognize it in the eyes of those you meet. You see, this is why they're called gifts! Your unique gifts, your unique talents, your unique potential are your loving contributions to this world. Gifts nicely wrapped up in the shape of you, and so very, very much appreciated by those receiving them. You're the gift! Yes!

Don't you see? At the end of this life, if you happen to experience a slow journey toward your death by sickness or age, as you move toward the end of your life, it will be crystal clear to you (if it wasn't already before then) that what matters most to us all is our heart to heart connections with others. Our relationships are what make us come alive! This is what makes us feel this gorgeous flow of energy, love, and joy. This is what matters most to us all, to authentically connect with others. This is our most precious gift to one another: to share, connect, reach out, and express ourselves.

At the core of us all is love. Love, compassion, joy, authenticity, and power are at the core of all of us. Yet at times we forget. At times, we struggle to remember who we are and to remember our brilliance. That's why we need to remind each other. That's why we need each other. That's why you're needed! That's why your gift, your story, and your services (paid or free) are so needed, each and every day of your life. You're needed by others! In the same way that you need others.

We all need and long for a sense of deep connectedness. We need to feel seen. We need to feel loved. We need to be reminded how precious we are, how appreciated we are at all times, regardless of any mistakes we might make along the way. You're precious, and when you recognize this in yourself, you'll remind others of their preciousness to an even greater extent. Allow yourself to truly see your beauty and brilliance. Allow yourself to be loving, forgiving, and loyal to yourself.

You've come here to shine! You've come here to share the brilliance of you: all your unique ideas, your thoughts, your loving energy, and your compassion. Share it! Express it. Be all of you. That's who you came here to be, to be embraced by life in your fullness. Be the lighthouse that you were born to be! Be the authentic and loving powerhouse that you've come here to be. Keep on shining, each and every day. Fill yourself up and share your overflow. Share it with your energy, with your outstanding creativity and your innate leadership skills. You know that true leaders lead the way with love, empowerment, and compassion. You know that true leaders believe in their tribe and have genuine compassion for one another. Our genuine hearts lead the way for us all. Go out and embrace the world with your authenticity, love, creativity, uplifting playfulness, and joy!

Your life and your experiences are unique. You may think: "Who am I to share my story? What is unique about my way? Have not my story about my experiences been told already, over and over by thousands of others?" It sure has. However, you with the combination of your experiences, the individuals within your story, your life struggles, challenges, how you overcome your struggles, and the lessons that you've learned all blend together into a unique and inspiring narrative. Because of this combination being unique, it offers a new perspective—your perspective. It may be a similar experience and a similar conclusion, yet it's your unique voice with your nuances. Your way of sharing it, your way of packaging it into a narration, a service, a product, or a way of living is completely unique.

You can share your story and serve others as an entrepreneur, or you can do this as a family member or a tribe member. Whichever way you choose to go about it, make sure to fill yourself up, be true to yourself and to your own needs, and then share that story of yours. Tell it. Your unique voice is so precious and so needed in this world of ours.

Think about it. When you're in some sort of crisis or difficult situation somehow, you look for help, don't you? In various ways. It could be a product, a service, a book, a family member, a song, or somebody who has experienced something similar. You look for it. You search for it. You search for hope and a solution instead of focusing on the problem. Trust that your experience and your story is that very solution that another person needs right now. So, in showing up for yourself authentically, you invite others to do the same. You inspire others. You show the possibilities that are available to them as well.

The sharing, serving, and being of service is in line with all the previous chapters in this book. You're a caring, compassionate person who wishes to contribute to others. That's at the core of who you are. If you follow these steps, to stay true to yourself and allow for more of you to take the ownership of your life, then you're in the best position to continue to serve others. You may continue to serve others in the same way you've always done. You may adjust it or up-level it somehow. Whatever way feels true at the core of you is the right way to go about it. As you make sure to fill yourself up first, you serve others from an entirely new place within. One that's abundant. One that's effortless. One that's your full potential, your ever-growing potential.

The major part of your journey in life has involved a rediscovery of yourself and your authenticity. You're rediscovering who you are without all the expectations, labels, facades, and masks that has been placed upon so many of us by society, families, schools, employers, friends and ourselves. Not all of those imposing ideas are intentional, nor are you aware of them occurring at all times. Know that all the things that you long for in life point toward what you are already. You're longing to be more of who you truly are. You simply haven't been allowing for you to be fully seen and discovered earlier.

Luckily, this is changing with every brave step that you take. There is still more to explore and enjoy each and every moment as you experience this magical adventure of your life. You see, the things we long for are all connected to how we wish to feel inside. At the core of every wish lies a hope for a better-feeling experience. How you feel about something is always entirely up to you. So the choice is yours at all times. How do you wish to feel? Will you allow for yourself to feel that better feeling emotion even before the outer circumstances matches your wishes? Will you allow for yourself to truly feel the freedom, love, and joy that's already available to you right now? You're so worthy of this and more. Now and always. Trust it. Feel it. Embrace it. It's already yours to choose.

The heart beats within your body, constantly reminding you of the miracle that you're here to experience: the miracle of being alive for this precious moment in time. You've been given a gift, this life of yours. You're allowed to use it with all your heart in the direction that you long to walk, regardless if it may not make sense to those around you.

You've come such a long way already. Know that there are so many others around you, that you not yet know of, who hope and pray for you to show up in their lives. They need you to share your story. They hope for you to embrace your dream in the way that you're doing today. They long to learn more about you. Abundantly share your life experience and your visions on life. Others long for your inspiring authenticity as it will provide an encouraging spark within to embark upon their own journey to embrace their truth and potential more fully.

Reflect in your journal.

♥ *TELL YOUR STORY* ♥

Create a timeline dating from when you were born up until today. Above the timeline, chart out major events and memories in your life that bring you joy and gratitude.

Below the timeline, chart out your major challenges, traumas, and setbacks in life. No need to dig deeper into them emotionally right now, simply *name* them. Allow whatever feelings that may arise to simply be there.

What do you know today that would have been beneficial for yourself to know back then? Write your insights and lessons down. Write it as if you were writing it to your younger versions of yourself. This is what others in similar situations most need to hear from you now. You're a provider of hope, truth, and inspiration. You always have been and always will be.

Think about it for a while. There are so many expectations placed upon us. As we go to school, we're expected to learn, to understand, to grow, and to do so in a specific format or else we will be labeled unqualified and consequently not fitting into the norm. There's been an ongoing process of restraints being placed upon you and your soul, and you've accepted this in the past.

Now you know better. Now you feel your freedom. You feel your unlimited potential and your unlimited options in your life. It's your life; it has been given to you specifically. You're free to climb the mountains and explore the valleys. You're free to rest by the rivers. You're free to indulge in the ever-flowing love that surrounds you at all times. You're so precious! You're so loved.

Life is constantly embracing you, showering you with opportunities, love, and connections. Life is constantly providing you with heart-to-heart encounters with other beautiful souls. Keep your eyes wide open, to see, notice, and embrace all the opportunities available to you. Keep your eyes open to proudly see and embrace your ever-growing potential. Notice how far you've come. Look back to those times when you struggled. See how much you've overcome already. See how profoundly you've contributed to others.

If you were to go back into that specific time and place when you struggled the most in life, what would you've wanted that version of you to know? Isn't it reassuring to know that where you are today proves that you're safe? Where you are today proves that you made it. More than that, you're still growing, learning, and evolving. You made it, in spite of those challenging times in your life.

You telling your story of successfully making it through, will inspire so many others who are now in that position that you were in the past. You sharing your story is in a sense you reaching out your hand to those in the very same shoes that you were once struggling in. You sharing your story is such a loving gesture of showing that "I'm here for you. I see you. I feel you. I know your pain. I know your struggle. I feel it. I have been there and I made it through. I'm still making process. I'm here for you." It's such a moving and loving thing to do. It's what you've been doing all along your entire life: you've been reaching your compassionate hand out to others. Doing so now, reaching your hand out to others in the expanded and energy-filled version of you, is inspiring beyond words. You now glow from within.

Imagine a candlelight in a windy environment. You place your hands around that flame to protect it from the challenging wind. As the wind gradually fades, the light and the flame survives. As you slowly remove your hands, the light gently becomes more and more visible. In a sense, this is what you've been doing in your times of struggle. You've been protecting your own light. You've not been visible in your full light at those points in time, as you've been turning inward, striving to cope, to understand, and survive. You've hidden yourself a bit from the world.

This is what we often do: We withdraw in times of trouble. It's part of this sense of shame; we wish to be successful at all times. Well, all of us, struggle at times with various things in life, at nearly all times. We all face various challenges of different proportions. There is always something to evolve, something to develop and endure. Even at times of seeming perfection, accidents can occur that will potentially evoke so much pain and sorrow, at times even overwhelming devastation. It's part of life. Life is never predictable in that sense.

So, this habit of withdrawing from the world serves a purpose. It provides us with a space and time to lick our wounds and to regain our strength. In those moments, when we slowly begin to rise again, to have someone inspiring standing in front of us is truly priceless. It really doesn't matter if this is a friend, a celebrity, a stranger, an author, a book, a movie, or whatever it might be. What matters is that empowering feeling that's being evoked within us. To have an empowering vision and role model right in front of us, someone standing tall as we're making those first movements to rise again, is absolutely life-changing. It's priceless, because that person, movie, book, film, or group of people are the evidence that what we're striving toward is actually possible.

We've all used this method. We've all found something to hold on to at times of despair or hopelessness. It could be an uplifting song, a picture of a loved one or a painting, simply something that evokes that extra sparkle within us to keep moving and keep going forward. We need something to remind us to keep believing during times of despair and challenges. This is how you can serve the world. You sharing your story, you making your dreams and visions come to life, is your gift to all your loving brothers and sisters out there in the world. We're all connected. We're all contributing to each other. Let us make that contribution an awesome one by bringing our full potential into the world, by allowing our full capacity of love and compassion to contribute to one another.

By being compassionate with one another and ourselves at the same time, we help make this world a better place, together, one moment at the time. It all begins with you. Each loving gesture, each loving service help create a better place for us all. One drop at the time. Consistently. One drop at the time will gradually fill the bowl that was once somewhat hollow. Keep contributing. Keep contributing from a place of you being filled up, from a place of you feeling passionate and authentic in every way. Let us create an awesome life experience by maximizing our love toward ourselves and others. Together, we rise.

As you share your story, you're very likely to receive heartwarming response from others who have felt the same way: others who have been through similar experiences or longed to express themselves more openly as regards similar subjects. You'll likely notice several of your friends and relatives opening up to you and expressing how they too have similar stories that long to be shared in a loving, safe space. You telling your story will result in you being more open and secure with who you are. Simultaneously, you'll be inspiring others, strangers as well as those close to you, to express more of who they truly are. It's a win-win.

To own your voice, potential, and authenticity in an ever-expanding way is the biggest service you can give yourself and the world. In sharing your story and owning your voice and your unique potential, you'll feel so alive, joyful, and energized without really making an effort. You're simply being you! Period. You're simply being you.

There you go! Yes, that's all there is to it. You're here to be all of you, as simple as that. You're here to taste and enjoy whatever you wish to order from the menu of life. You're here to enjoy all of life in the very unique way that's true for you, the way that gives you that extra sparkle, energy boost, and super excitement! To do that is to give yourself the pleasure of waking up to feeling "Yes, another day! Yes, bring it on!" You'll face whatever challenge or project that's ahead of you with new energy and with new vibrant commitment to yourself and to those that you're here to connect with.

The world doesn't consist of billions of people for no reason. We're here to connect, to unite, and to build loving, vibrant, energy-giving communities together through connections. We're here to see and feel seen. We're here to be fully alive and to truly live in passion, joy, authenticity, and expansion. As you show the world more of you, as you tell your story and share it, it opens up new opportunities and experiences that will live forever in your heart. These moments will touch both you and others deeply. This is what we all thrive upon, those rewarding memorable moments of love, authenticity, and connection. As you unite with your truth, you will thrive. As you radiate in your truth, your genuine tribe will find you.

Life is not about putting your own needs aside for the sake of somebody else, no. It's about you owning your needs, meeting them, asking for help when needed, and reaching out and serving others when needed and possible. Life is about being there for both yourself and for each other. We need to nurture both ourselves and others so we can grow and thrive together.

Rest in your brilliance. Trust your awesomeness. Know that you're worth loving, that your perspective on life is valuable and longed for. Know that your view of the world is needed: your sense of humor, your struggles, your pain as well as your joy. Your authentic expression moves mountains and touches others deeply. Your authentic expression invites people in. It invites them into your miraculous and contagious beauty. Trust that whatever you've been through, whatever struggles that have brought you to your knees in despair, are the very things that have given you a depth and a deeper understanding for life. These events have given you a deeper understanding for the struggles of others so that you're better able to connect more deeply with those who need it the most right now.

There is a beautiful story, written by Tove Jansson (1914– 2001), that's called "The Invisible Child." It depicts a girl who has been neglected. She has experienced harshness to such an extent that she dimmed herself into invisibleness. As she moves in with a new family, she begins to feel noticed, appreciated, and included.

Gradually, she is able to allow herself to be seen again and become the fully visible and naturally joyful girl that she was born to be. Beautiful illustration through story, isn't it?

One important way of connecting with each other is through the stories of our hearts, the ones that we carry with us. Some stories are even told in pure silence as you gaze into the eyes of another beautiful being. We're able to express our stories in so many creative ways: through a silent gaze, through an embrace, through dancing, through a theatrical performance, through music, singing, through holding a speech, or writing a book, etc. A story can be told through holding the hand of another. Our bodies speak a language of their own, consciously as well as unconsciously. Embrace your creative and authentic storyteller within.

Keep embracing the beauty of who you are. Keep embracing the beauty of those you meet. You're so loved. You're so precious. For you to be able to see the miraculous gift that you are to the world is my wish for you. See your beauty. Feel it. Enjoy it. Share it. You were born to shine, friend. Your beautiful heart shines so brightly. Your beautiful heart shines so loudly, even in the silence. Trust it. Trust the song in your heart that sings the tune of your truth. As you already know, there is life-changing magic in truth. Trust your magic. I believe in you, and I always will. Keep allowing your heart to shine freely. I'd like to thank you for giving yourself and the world the gift of all of you. With all my heart, thank you for being you. You contribute immensely to this world by being you. If only you knew how many hearts you've touched already. Priceless, really. Keep shining, friend. You light up the world with your loving eyes. Let them shine!

Remember that there are already those longing for you to bravely show up so that they can be brave too. So, where, how, and when will you begin to tell your story?

At the end of your life, how will the world be different because you were born?

Your Life Purpose

To live a meaningful life, serve others by doing what you love.
It is really as simple as that. Share your unique gift, friend.
You are needed.

About Helena Goodwill

Helena Goodwill is an intuitive coach, Reiki Master, and artist. She holds an MA in English literature (from the University of Stockholm, Sweden) and has also studied to become a social worker. All in all, she has enjoyed seven years of university studies. To lovingly support others in *seeing* and *living* their full potential is her big passion in life. Many of her paintings aim to inspire others to make more room for playfulness, authenticity, love, creativity and their dreams in their everyday life. (All images in this book have been created by Helena).

Helena was born an optimist. As a baby, she would wake up with a joyful morning scream, as if enthusiastically celebrating the gift of a new day and the gift of life. Helena is a free spirit who is dedicated to abundantly share the love, joy, compassion, and wisdom within her. Luckily, through the years, she has grown to realize that her love also needs to be shared with herself as well, that self-love is, in fact, a prerequisite for being able to fully embrace this vision of hers.

Like so many others, she has encountered various traumas in life. In her youth, she experienced sexual harassment from an unknown predator who kept harassing and stalking her for eleven years through phone calls, pornographic material of children delivered by post, sexually condescending letters, orders of various sexual contents in her name, and occasionally ringing the doorbell when she was alone at home in the dark nights when her parents were away, singing in a choir. More than having lived through these sexual harassments as a young girl, she has also experienced rape, domestic violence, and abuse in adulthood. Already as a child, she was always striving for forgiveness and to set herself and the other free. This is her mentality today as well.

In past relationships, she surrendered her needs in attempts to make others happy and content, whomever they were: a coworker, friend, stranger, or relative. With time, she grew to understand that another's happiness didn't have to exist at the expense of her own. She grew to understand that loving herself and nurturing her dreams and visions was, in fact, her major mission in life. Knowing this has helped Helena to excel from previous patterns into her new way of living in which she feeds her soul and simultaneously more easily pours love, understanding, and compassion into her connections with others.

In her early thirties, while being a single parent and studying at the University of Stockholm, Helena began bleeding internally. Suffering from pain, too embarrassed to seek help and somehow hoping it would all heal by itself, she kept bleeding for more than a month from her gut. When she eventually went to the hospital, she was diagnosed with colitis, a form of IBD (irritable bowel disease), which her doctor told her was a chronic disease that she would have to live with for the rest of her life. She was given various medicines, but none of them helped cure her completely, as the bleeding kept returning again and again over the coming months.

A friend of hers more or less forced her to go seek the guidance of his friend, who was into alternative medicine, to overcome her painful symptoms. With lots of resistance, she did. This man told her that she had intuitive skills that she ignored, which was the root cause of her gut problems. They began cooperating, and he helped her realize how gifted she was. He would give her the name of someone he knew and ask her to describe the person. Not knowing whom the person was, she began describing the person in detail, and as it turned out, each description was accurate. She had accurately described this man's family members without knowing it beforehand. The man even asked her to close her eyes as he placed a book in her hands and requested that she describe what type of book it was. She then felt a sensation in her chest, as well as a sensation at the top of her head, and she could feel a connecting bond between these two sensations in her body. As she opened her eyes, she saw that the book she was holding in her hands was *Las Relaciones entre el Yo y el Inconsciente* (*The Relations between the Ego and the Unconscious*) by Carl Gustav Jung. She was blown away upon seeing this. Still not feeling fully comfortable with her intuitive skills, she tried her best to be as "normal" as possible. To be accepted by others. To fit in. To fully accept and express this side of herself was an internal journey that required a couple of years to pass. Today, Helena is proud of her gifts and uses them daily with her clients, family, and friends, as well as on her own.

Helena is devoted to acknowledging and cherishing the innate beauty in those she comes in contact with. To remind others of their excellence so they can set themselves free to live their truth, that's what sets her soul on fire. She loves seeing others trust their brilliance and spread their wings in the direction in which they long to soar. Seeing others shine while expressing their genuine truth, love, and joy fills her heart with pure bliss.

Helena lives with her precious son Anthony in Stockholm, Sweden. She is creating her life based on the truth that lives in her heart, a truth that sings that we're all free and meant for greatness. In her embrace, be it through words or a physical hug, you feel safe to be you. You feel seen, acknowledged and loved for who you truly are. Upon receiving that experience, others relax into their own truth. Upon connecting with Helena, others allow themselves to enjoy their freedom, to reach for more, to give more, to serve more, and to nurture themselves more. Helena is genuinely compassionate with others, which is an experience that transforms a doubting heart. Love is by far the most precious contribution we can give one another.

Helena contributes to this world by truly seeing and touching others on a deeper level. For those who are ready to face the truth of their longing, the root cause of their perceived suffering, Helena is devoted to providing a loving, safe space for them all.

Breathe a sigh of relief. Giggle with excitement in your free expression of yourself. Through her writing, courses, artwork, coaching, and various events, Helena is here to serve the world with her love and wisdom in various ways so that we can all live genuinely happy, energized and love-filled lives that make a difference to ourselves and the world.

Through her own life experiences, Helena has been in the darkest of valleys and returned back to the top. Because of this, she is able to hold your hand with a strong, pure conviction that will inevitably bring hope back into your heart. Her presence reminds you that forgiveness and liberation are always available and possible. She is a living example that you too can reconnect with that pure source of joy and love within you.

www.helenagoodwill.com

TETRIS TAUGHT
ME THAT WHEN
YOU TRY
TO FIT IN YOU
DISAPPEAR

Helena Goodwill in one
of her favorite shirts

CPSIA information can be obtained
at www.ICGtesting.com
Printed in the USA
BVHW031449180220
572693BV00008B/25